THE COMPANY THAT BOUGHT THE BOARDWALK

THE COMPANY THAT BOUGHT THE BOARDWALK

**A REPORTER'S STORY OF
HOW RESORTS INTERNATIONAL
CAME TO ATLANTIC CITY**

GIGI MAHON

RANDOM HOUSE NEW YORK

Library of Congress Cataloging in Publication
Data
Mahon, Gigi.
The company that bought the boardwalk.
Includes index.
1. Resorts International. 2. Gambling—New
Jersey—Atlantic City. I. Title.
HV6721.N48M33   338.7′61795   80-5301
ISBN 0-394-50978-1

Manufactured in the United States of America
9 8 7 6 5 4 3 2
First Edition

**To Alan Abelson,
editor and friend**

ACKNOWLEDGMENTS

My thanks to:

New Jersey Attorney General John Degnan
and his staff, especially press aide Tom
Cannon, for hours on the phone and always
finding me a desk,

Chief of the New Jersey Division of Criminal
Justice, Ed Stier,

Fellow *Barron's* editors Kate Welling and
Tom Donlan, for their input,

Lawyer Bob Sack, for his legal—and editorial
—reading,

My agent, John Ware, and my editor,
Charlotte Mayerson,

Finally, Bruce Hallettt, for his constant moral
support.

THE COMPANY THAT BOUGHT
THE BOARDWALK

PROLOGUE

On a sweltering afternoon in the summer of 1977, I strolled the Boardwalk of Atlantic City and thought how nothing had changed. The smells were familiar: salt air mingled with hot dogs and wood and tar from the beach. The people were the same, old, mostly—old women in Bermuda shorts and straw hats, old men sitting on benches or riding on the tram that rolls up and down the six-mile stretch of planking. There were more than the usual number of burned-out buildings. Arson, for profit, was more popular than ever. There was a stir in the still, wet air when police broke up a gang of teenagers who were doing—no one knew what.

Up at the Chalfonte-Haddon Hall Hotel, a handful of construction men labored through the heat, a renovation under way. But for that, the façades of the old hotels remained as they had for years, sagging, gray, like the faces of the people who sat on the Boardwalk day after day. It was the same Atlantic City, long ago duchess of resorts, now an arthritic and dowdy dowager trying desperately to cling to her past. A bag of worn-out bricks on splintered pilings.

But despite its appearance, things *had* changed, in less than a year, in ways you couldn't see from the Boardwalk. Behind the scenes, as close by as City Hall, as far away as the state capital of Trenton, and even further, in the Bahamas and Europe and Japan, a new life was being planned for Atlantic City. It had to do with gambling. Events had occurred that would send waves crashing up the New Jersey shore, through the state, then rippling outward, into other states, a country.

The big event: passage, in November of 1976, of a referendum in New Jersey that legalized casino gambling in Atlantic City. And with it there emerged on the scene Resorts International, a company that had arrived first, had set the tone, the precedents, and later would be joined by scores of others. Together they would set into motion a maelstrom of forces that were rich and powerful and corrupt. They promised jobs and a reborn Atlantic City, but they didn't say that in the process, public officials would be compromised, blacks and Hispanics and the elderly would be forced from their homes, new avenues of opportunity would be thrown open to organized crime and the price of law enforcement would skyrocket. Good law enforcement people would grow disillusioned and leave. And in the end the only clear winners would be the companies that had marched through, like Sherman through Georgia, and walked away with a state.

The people wouldn't notice at first. They had been lulled, cajoled with promises of lower taxes, new jobs and social progress. The men who represented them had been lulled, too, sometimes with altruism, sometimes not. Throughout it all, their governor would tell them they had nothing to fear.

It had not begun in Atlantic City and it would probably not end there, and whatever part greed and corruption played in that arena, it had always been, and would always be, present in equal measure wherever gambling was an issue or a reality.

In the United States, Las Vegas wrote the history books on legal casinos, and it wasn't a very noble past upon which to build a future. Modern-day Las Vegas, "the Strip," the show girls, the big-time entertainment—it was all the brainchild of Bugsy Siegel, a mobster. When he was murdered by his own associates for sins of greed, there were plenty like him to take his place. Nevada knew, everyone knew, the men in control were shady characters, but they chose to allow it. How could you throw out the people who were responsible for your success? they reasoned. Besides, the mob had the gambling expertise, knew how to make money. They knew how not to get ripped off by their customers and employees. Without the mob, goes the story, Las Vegas would never have made it.

Today in Nevada they say that all of that has changed. Conservatively suited lawyers sit in tasteful offices where regulation takes place. They explain that once, Nevada tapped organized crime know-how for all it was worth, and when the state learned all it needed to know, it got tough. It threw the bums out, vanquished them. Then it set up bodies of regulation that were honest, independent and staffed by men whose only concern was that Nevada be clean.

After they told you that, as you were leaving their office, they would offer you free tickets to the shows at the casinos. The casinos provided them, they would say. And a year or two later, they would leave the place of regulation and show up on the payroll at some casino, or they would go to law firms and their clients would be the casinos they had been so "independent" of months before.

What they said had never been true. The mob was still there. It had gone further underground, perhaps, hidden its interests better, but it still flourished. Even as the decade of the seventies closed, casino scandals were monthly occurrences. The purges of recent history have often come only after Nevada has been embarrassed into action by the press or by law enforcement actions at the federal level or in other jurisdictions.

Over the years, things have gotten worse. Gaming officials

have shown little interest in the recommendations of the state investigators. The gaming commission chairman, Harry Reid, is a man who knows politics. Nevada is a one-industry state, and it is not good politics to alienate the industry. The chairman has done little to alienate the industry.

Greed and politics are compatible where the stakes are high and where the stakes are cash. After Nevada and before New Jersey, other states had seen a push to legalize casinos. In New Hampshire the idea gained the support of an ornery governor, Meldrim Thomson, who wanted to avoid passing an income tax, and a notorious newspaper publisher, William Loeb, of the Manchester *Union Leader,* a man with a multimillion-dollar line of credit from the Teamsters Central States Pension Fund, a long-time supporter of casino interests.

In Florida a casino vote was soundly defeated in 1975, then again in 1978—in the latter year on tales of what havoc was being wrought in New Jersey, and on strong, monied opposition from race-track interests and from a governor who said surely there must be a better way for a state to raise revenues. But even there it's a live issue. Miami Beach is too apt a spot, with its hulking hotels with their huge lobbies, with its reputation as a spa for organized crime. The drive has begun again. A staunch anti-casino law enforcement official has been ousted by a superior who is not of that persuasion. Is it coincidence? Already the money has begun flooding in. This time it will be harder to stave it off.

In New York the governor, Hugh Carey, at first nixed the notion, then deemed it okay if state-run, then turned around and encouraged approval of privately owned casinos, then invited anyone's guess as to what, exactly, his position was. And even as reports trickled in of mob rub-outs over the dividing of the spoils in Atlantic City, Hugh Carey reported that the governor of New Jersey had told him everything was going just fine. Brendan Byrne said it was a rousing success, no problems, and he, Hugh Carey, had believed him.

But where to put the casinos? The Catskill Mountains, perhaps, where for years, it was rumored, the mob had been accumulating property in drooling anticipation. Or maybe the Hamptons or Montauk or Saratoga. The mayor of New York, Ed Koch, was enthusiastic. "Why?" someone asked him. Why not? was the reply. He had to meet the competitive threat from the state next door. Surely people didn't believe that where tourists were concerned, the United Nations and the Statue of Liberty and the shops and theaters were any match for casinos. Besides, New Yorkers should have the right to lose money in their own state; they shouldn't have to go across state lines to do it.

Other states—California, Connecticut, Hawaii, Massachusetts, Pennsylvania and Vermont, to name just a few—are considering the idea. A man trying to push casinos in Ocean City, Maryland, explained why:

"For two years Maryland had this here lottery, and it's making a lot of money for the state. So we want gambling in Ocean City. We have a tough mayor and he's been against it for years, but lately he's done this little flip-flop and said he'd consider it and could change his mind. Now, this is a tough mayor. Yesterday he told a corps of engineers to go to hell, so you know he's a tough mayor, and when he changes his mind, it means something."

Of course, the man continued, there were the usual weak hearts among the locals, but there were only twelve hundred of so of them. There were many thousands of absentee owners, himself included, and they liked the idea because property values would skyrocket. The locals were scared about prostitution and machine guns. Never mind, said the man, we already have prostitution: "In summer down there, the kids are wild.

Promiscuously, there's a lot going on down there." Anyway, they weren't talking on a grand scale. Nothing like Vegas. "A lot of slot machines, maybe a few first-class casinos."

On paper it looked good. On paper you couldn't see the costs, just as on the Boardwalk that August afternoon you couldn't see that behind the scenes, Resorts International was leaning over the shoulders of the legislators, whose palms clutched pens that drafted legislation that would give Resorts a one-year, $200 million head start on the competition. Paul Volpe and other Canadian mob figures were invisible too, but they were pouring tens of millions of dollars into Atlantic City real estate. A hidden war was emerging among organized-crime factions over control of everything from casinos to vending machines. It was thought that three big-gun fatalities by early 1980 were directly related to Atlantic City gambling—mobsters Tony Russo, Carmine Galante and Angelo Bruno, all murdered.

There was action, too, in the stock market. The stocks of gambling companies would soar and later plummet. Before it was over, professionals and casino executives would line their already padded pockets and small investors would lose millions of dollars. But you didn't know that then. All you knew was that the governor of New Jersey had given the most dramatic speech of his career. "Keep your filthy hands out of Atlantic City and keep the hell out of our state!" he told the mob. "Organized crime is not welcome." And the people of New Jersey believed he meant it. It was the convenient thing to do.

What follows is the story of how it all began, and how it happened in one state, and how one company, with a shady past and a questionable present, stacked the deck and dealt itself a winning hand. But it could have been another state and it could have been another company. Odds are that soon it will be.

PART ONE

SLEUTHING

CHAPTER ONE

It was a good time to get out of New York. The city, that August of 1977, was melting in the grip of an oppressive heat wave, and the best of all worlds, for a reporter, would be an assignment to somewhere more temperate, someplace where the trade winds blew and the water was swimmable, someplace like Paradise Island. And that was the assignment I drew, for *Barron's Financial Weekly*. My story had another locale, too, also by the sea, but somewhat less exotic: Atlantic City, New Jersey. The story was Resorts International.

Of the company, all I knew was this: When the voters of New Jersey approved the legalization of casinos in Atlantic City in 1976, Resorts International was first on the scene. In fact, it had been there even before the referendum—grabbing up cheap property that would later become prime; hiring well-connected lawyers to ease the way; unleashing a construction crew on what would become the grandest and gaudiest, biggest and best, richest casino to hit the shores of the Garden State. To be all of that, it had to be first.

Of course, the story of Resorts International did not begin in Atlantic City; it began on other shores. It was a company with strange and ominous origins. It changed overnight from

Mary Carter Paint Company, a paint manufacturer and re-tailer, into Resorts International, a casino empire. It dealt openly with the mob, yet boasted its own in-house intelligence force, which sold its services to other companies to help them be free of crime influence. Resorts usually got what it wanted —free, if it could—through persuasion, flattery or, failing those, through other means, like supplying hookers or molding testimony or paying off whoever it was necessary to. It paid a former public relations man over a million dollars on the condi-tion that he *not* talk. The company's stock pulsated wildly on the strength of every new scheme, darting upward in the wake of artfully produced press releases, ever enriching manage-ment. And once, when it had assets in the low millions and burdensome debt, it tried to take over a billion-dollar airline.

It was a company, then, where little happened in an uninter-esting or even "normal" manner. Employees didn't simply quit or get fired. They had to flee the island because they were caught with drugs and guns. Or, in the case of one employee, because a bag of marijuana was found in his car, but, as it turned out, bearing the fingerprints of another employee, who went to jail rather than say who had made him do it. An executive's wife didn't just die, she committed suicide in a company-owned apartment and lay dead for days before her body was found. An executive's home wasn't just robbed, it was burglarized by men in stocking masks who were interested not just in cash and jewels but in documents too. An amazing array of friends and associates and even relatives ended up wanted for or convicted of some crime or another.

Hotel guests were the usual honeymooning Ohioans, but also visiting from time to time were Nixon and Rebozo and Vesco and Kissinger and Cornfeld. Paradise Island would har-bor Howard Hughes and the Shah of Iran and a host of mod-ern-day pirates on the lam from one government or another. Indeed, they often helped steer the course of their guests' lives.

Howard Hughes was hustled from Las Vegas by a posse from Resorts' security subsidiary, Intertel. They had been hired to protect his casinos and him, but while under their protective wing, he would die a needless death, with five hypodermic needles, vestiges of a decades-long addiction to codeine, embedded in his arms.

But I knew none of that in August, only that somewhere it had to be cooler. My first stop was Atlantic City.

CHAPTER TWO

There are lots of towns on the New Jersey shore, and lots of boardwalks—Point Pleasant, Asbury Park, Spring Lake—but the one I remember visiting as a child was the one recognized from California to New York as *the* Boardwalk, with the capital B. Atlantic City. It was wider and longer, lined with restaurants, fancy hotels, souvenir shops and nightclubs on one side and big tarry beaches on the other. There were piers jutting out to sea that were crowded with amusements and rides and spinning wheels and haunted houses and ladies who turned into apes. The Boardwalk was Miss America and salt-water taffy and rolling wicker chairs.

Once it had even been glamorous. It was a playground for the rich as well as the masses, a Fifth Avenue by the sea, a place to stroll, to people-watch, to hear Benny Goodman play. And it was a city of many firsts: Easter parade, Ferris wheel, motion picture and color picture postcard. Atlantic City drew the hordes with big bands and big hotels and a big boisterous time. It was alive. But there came a point, which almost nobody noticed, when the life began seeping out of it.

By 1976, many of the people who were still loyal had no other choice. They were poor or old or both; they couldn't afford to leave. Miss America was still there too—oddly appropriate. The contest's image was as fixed to Atlantic City as the smiles were to the contestants' faces. But the hotels, once in the vanguard of oceanfront, skyscraping luxury, no longer enticed tourists. Travelers, spoiled by the bland comforts of Hilton or the disinfected sameness of Holiday Inn, could not be lured to places where the bathroom was a commute down the hall. Many of the hotels shut, and there they stood, tired old white elephants, humiliated, a symbol of everything that had gone wrong. You couldn't blame Atlantic City for trying to find a way out of its misery. You could even understand when the way it found was casinos.

After years of machinations, after a referendum calling for statewide gambling was defeated in 1974, promoters tried again. This time, casinos would be confined to Atlantic City. A million-dollar public relations effort was mounted. The chief lobby was the Committee to Rebuild Atlantic City, the biggest contributor Resorts International. Hundreds of thousands of dollars were poured into advertisements, packaged sincerity, an appeal to people's better instincts. Here was a way to save Atlantic City—a novel tool for urban renewal, they called it— and it wouldn't be a bother to the rest of the state. It would help the old folks—the elderly were the intended beneficiaries of other people's misfortunes at the tables. (That is, after the casino operators had taken the lion's share.) Voting against casinos was like sending your mother to work in a mine.

Blacks and Hispanics constituted a big voting bloc in New Jersey, and that is why they were appealed to. A charismatic black California politician, Willie Brown, was imported. He was paid at least $5,000 plus expenses to fill his brothers and sisters in on how much good they would be doing themselves if only they voted "yes." And on election day, thousands upon thousands of dollars of "street money" were filtered through the city and state. What was it for? They said it paid for babysitters and taxicabs and buses to help people to the polls. But while the amounts—at least some of them—were reported, no one ever explained why, exactly, for example, a man named Hector Rodriguez, a Puerto Rican community leader, was paid over $10,000 worth of "election day expenses." You had to report only that you had dispensed it to one group or one politician, but not what they had done with it.

It all paid off, and how. On November 2, 1976, pro-casino forces recovered spectacularly from their former defeats. The lobbying effort Resorts International had been waging on and off for nearly a decade succeeded. Citizens of New Jersey okayed casinos in Atlantic City by an overwhelming margin. Overwhelming margin? You could almost see the consciousness of state legislators being collectively raised. Casinos were suddenly good politics. The day after the vote, there was rejoicing on the Boardwalk. The country was celebrating an anniversary; Atlantic City, a rebirth.

By the time I got there, nine months later, the dancing in the streets had given way to the humdrum everyday reality of planning. Legislation had been enacted earlier that summer. Leonard Ronco, head of the governor's Office of Casino Policy, said he was enthusiastic. Atlantic City would set an example —it would be clean. They had made sure the laws were stricter than in Nevada. New Jersey would be a model for gambling everywhere.

Reese Palley was similarly enthusiastic. Reese Palley was the name of a man and a store, and both were Atlantic City landmarks. The store was the only one left on the Boardwalk that hawked pricier goods, Boehm birds, china and crystal. It was in contrast to its neighbors, many of whom filled their windows with T-shirts proclaiming things like MY PARENTS WENT TO ATLANTIC CITY AND ALL THEY BROUGHT ME WAS THIS LOUSY T-SHIRT.

Palley was a flamboyant, middle-aged, gray-goateed, Porsche-driving entrepreneur. He was the one Boardwalk shopkeeper who was foresighted enough to see that Atlantic City's bright new future might not include him. So he took action. He and some partners bought the hotel his store was in, the Marlborough-Blenheim. That hotel, more than any other, said "Boardwalk" to a lot of old-timers. Planted in its middle, facing the Boardwalk, was a large gray rotunda, a mosque-type Arabian nights affair.

Palley was less sanguine than Ronco on the prospects for excluding organized crime. Of course they would be there, he told me. They follow the money. But look at the bright side. The numbers were incredible! Within a three-hundred-mile radius of Atlantic City, there were sixty million people! There were only twelve million within that radius of Las Vegas! Right there you had a killing!

In his conference room was a model of the future Marlborough-Blenheim Hotel—or whatever it would be called. It had glassy twin towers bearing no resemblance to their predecessor hotel. But there in the middle was the rotunda, allowed to stand, sentimental and secure, a reminder of the Atlantic City that once was. They wouldn't dream of tearing it down, Palley said. It was historic. The city fathers would never let them and he wouldn't have it any other way.

Months later, a deafening blast cracked the early-morning sky, and in seconds the rotunda was no more. By that time Palley would have sold the hotel to Bally Corporation, but that is getting ahead of the story. Right then, in August, there was only hope and excitement. Anyone could make a killing in casinos, Palley said. "It's a no-brains business."

CHAPTER THREE

A couple of days later, the story took me to the shores of Paradise Island, the Bahamas. I tried to imagine what the place must have looked like in the fifties, when it belonged to a Swede named Wenner-Gren. It was called Hog Island then, jarringly unromantic, but never would a paradise have been so aptly named. The sky was blue, the water green, the waves gentle, the sand white. The palm trees swayed, the natives smiled, all was according to island lore.

In the seventies you stood on the shores of Cabbage Beach, and try as you might to conjure up visions of loveliness, you could not ignore the oversized hotels, the well-greased poolside hamburgers, the well-greased American tourists. A small-scale Miami Beach. No paradise this.

I had called the president of Resorts International, Jack Davis, and made an appointment for a couple of days after I would arrive, leaving time to sleuth first, get background and a feel for the place. But the Bahamas were in the midst of elections, and government officials, a target for talks, were hard to pin down in more ways than one. When I finally did get hold of them, the language of the Bahamas came clear—or was it the international language of politicians?

"Yes, of course we will renew the license of Resorts International," one minister said, "that is, unless we have reason not to." And "Oh yes," said another, "they have done a fine job here as managers of a casino—that is, unless we find they have done otherwise."

The issue that year was whether Resorts International would retain control of its Paradise Island Casino or whether it would be forced to sell or whether, even, the casino would be expropriated. Black governments made white businessmen worry that way. And the government of the Bahamas had clearly stated that as of 1978, it would own the casinos. Its terms were not yet divulged. So the uncertainty as to the fate of Resorts International in Atlantic City was matched by that in the Bahamas. Everyone wanted to know more.

Toward that end, on a Friday morning I ventured down to the lobby of the Paradise Island Hotel, walked through a short corridor connecting the hotel to the casino, then through the casino—dimly lit by chandeliers, defying the tropical white light outside—to another passageway leading to the Britannia Beach Hotel and, at the far end of the lobby, into the offices of Resorts International. I presented myself to a receptionist and announced my appointment with Jack Davis.

The receptionist motioned me to a waiting room, from which I could hear muffled voices that came from an adjoining office. They were male voices, and a man I assumed to be Davis was telling the other men a story. He used the word *"Barron's,"* a moment later they all laughed and then they left. Once they were out of sight, I was ushered in.

His office was on a corner, small but luxurious in its opulent tropical setting. There was a stereo, comfortable-looking furniture, a prime view of Paradise Lake. The office was above the pool of the Britannia Beach, and splashing sounds and sun-muted murmurs drifted through the open windows.

Davis was a man of about fifty, medium height, with close-to-the-head wavy brown hair. He had a tan that was deep, but no deeper than the opening in his shirt, which cleaved downward for several buttons. He was the kind of man who gave the impression of sporting jewelry against a hair-covered chest, even if he had neither jewelry nor hair. His face rivaled Rushmore for stony impassiveness. It was a book that refused to be read. He was cordial enough that morning, though, taking a pleasant tone, although the first thing he said was that he had bad news: "Yesterday afternoon the board of directors decided that we are no longer speaking to the press." He said, "There are a number of reasons why, but I can't say what they are." He added that while not singling anyone out, they were particularly not speaking to my magazine because "we just don't feel we can get a fair hearing in *Barron's.*"

He mentioned a *Barron's* columnist named "Abelman"—he meant Alan Abelson and I'd a feeling he knew it—who just that week had written disparagingly about Resorts International. (Now, it might have been less awkward for me if Abelson had not taken that particular week—when I was traveling to Paradise Island—to tackle that particular topic. But he was my managing editor, a nice man and a celebrated columnist who had planned that column before I planned my trip. Also, it was too late now.)

Then Davis said that "Abelman" was in cahoots with people who wanted to see the price of Resorts' stock go down, people who stood to make a lot of money if Resorts didn't do well. (It turned out to be a charge Resorts found convenient to level at many of its critics.) I told him it just wasn't so, then tried to figure out how I was going to justify my expense account when my interview had been a stonewall. I tried to direct the would-be interview. "Must be nice living in this climate," I said, "and by the way, is the Bahamian government going to throw you off the islands?" And, "This sure is a swell office with a nifty view, and while we're at it, what are your capital spending plans, where are you getting the dough, who's going to win the election and what will the company earn next year?" It didn't work. We chatted for a few minutes, but every time I asked something worth knowing, Davis would laugh and say that he was getting into something he was not allowed to talk about. So all I learned was the following:

• The government of the Bahamas is comprised of very reasonable people, fair in their dealings, good on their word. The relationship between Resorts International and the government had always been excellent. (It turned out that Resorts, and Davis in particular, had dealings with the top officials in the Bahamas that were so acrimonious as to at times all but bring the functioning of Paradise Island to a halt. The company would later use those bad relations as a part of their reason for having paid a publicity man over a million dollars—to say nothing of having handed out hundreds of thousands of dollars' worth of cash and gifts to a pride of lower-, middle- and upper-level customs officials, political parties and a minister or two.)

• The old Boardwalk hotel they had bought in Atlantic City, the Chalfonte-Haddon Hall, would be lovingly restored with the greatest care to its original prestige and polish. After all, they didn't want to come in and change the face and character of a town by ruining or tearing down a perfectly wonderful old building. (Translation: It's a lot cheaper to renovate a shabby old hotel than it is to put up a new one to the tune of $100 million plus. More important, if you only renovate, you save lots of time and gain a one-year, $200 million jump on the competition, which is forced—by legislation you had a large hand in crafting—to start from scratch.)

• What the press, and *Barron's* in particular, failed to realize was how very profitable gambling was. It was a real, lucrative business. (That was less than clear upon examination of Resorts' financial statements.) If I wanted to talk to an expert, why didn't I contact Walter Tyminski, the editor of a newsletter called *Rouge et Noir,* perhaps the foremost authority on gambling? (I later did contact Tyminski and he *was* knowledgeable, but by the time we spoke, he had become quite disapproving in print of Resorts' character and methods of operation. Resorts thus began trying to discredit him at every opportunity, accusing him of the same thing they accused *Barron's* of—trying to drive their stock price down.)

• Sorry as he was that he could not talk, what could he do to make my stay more comfortable? Reservations, perhaps, at the famed Cafe Martinique restaurant? (James Bond, the ever-discriminating, had dined there in *Thunderball.*) Could he pick up the tab for my airfare? My room? He'd be glad to. (As Humphrey Bogart might have said to Mary Astor, "You're good, you're real good." Wouldn't that be nice, months hence, for Resorts International to pull out of its corporate pocket proof that a *Barron's* reporter had all-expenses-paid-it on Paradise Island?)

I thanked him politely, declined and left.

I walked down to the beach, sat on the edge of the water, and a man nearby wearing a painter's cap struck up a conversation. He was German, he said, an engineer from Hamburg who came there every year. It was a relaxing place, he said, almost nothing to do. "The casino," he whispered, "is run by the Mafia."

"How do you know?"

"I can tell by their faces."

After a while we walked up to the casino, which was only sparsely populated. The afternoon sun was still bright outside, but inside, as in most casinos, there was no hint of the time or the temperature. The German pointed out the "Mafia types," mean-looking men overseeing the tables, thuglike. "I told you," he said with confidence. We watched the play for an hour or so, then I went back to my room and packed. I had decided by then that Jack Davis notwithstanding, I would not drop the story on Resorts International.

Back in New York, my managing editor, Alan Abelson, was predictably outraged. The more he thought about it, the madder he got. How dare Resorts International stand up *Barron's*? What were the mysterious reasons Jack Davis alluded to? Board of directors nothing. He said he had half a mind to call up Davis himself and give him what-for, and I told him I would just as soon he didn't. It would be like your mother calling a teacher who had crossed you. It would only prove you were a baby.

The story was still on. There followed weeks of searching through clips and court records and other documents, preparing a background on which to base questions for interviews. It didn't take long to realize that armies of ink-stained thumbs had already marched through these pages, that it was ground that had been trodden by many an intrepid investigative reporter—to say nothing of U.S. attorneys and district attorneys and Florida state attorneys and the FBI and the CIA and the IRS and the Justice Department and House and Senate committees and Watergate committees and private investigators. *Barron's* would not be the first to be intrigued, and mystified, by this company, and certainly not the last. It was a hard company to pin down—inscrutable. The cast of characters was huge. Personalities floated in and out of the story, leaving their mark, then fading away. Others clung on for the duration, involving themselves in everything the company touched.

For a reporter, unsubstantiated leads would wind up heading straight toward "the facts," while seemingly reliable accounts would turn out to be fiction. Loose ends would be hard to tie up, piles of notes would seem like pieces of a puzzle that couldn't be fitted together. Time and time again, there was a promise of an answer, or at least of a summing up, not only of the story of Resorts but of the inside story of New Jersey gambling—Abscam, New Jersey investigations, SEC investigations. Again and again, there would be hope that someone with the proper tools would solve the mysteries—or at least gather the strands together. So far, no one has done so.

CHAPTER FOUR

One person who presumably knew a lot about Resorts International was Huntington Hartford, a man whose name is associated with beautiful women, mansions, penthouse apartments and fantastic wealth, like Howard Hughes or J. Paul Getty. Hartford was a man of the eccentricity born of millions, one thought, a man fabled to have more money than he could possibly dispose of easily, but a man who nowadays, anyway, pleads poverty.

Someone put it this way: "Howard Hughes inherited mere millions from his father and turned it into billions. Huntington Hartford inherited millions and turned it into hundreds of thousands." The quote is not wholly accurate, but the point is well taken.

In print, more times than not, Hartford is "the A&P heir." That is where the money came from. Where it went was *Show* magazine, the Show Club, a New York museum that was supposed to rival the Museum of Modern Art, a modeling agency, a liquor store. All failed. Add to the list Paradise Island. Once he had that, too.

It was Hartford who bought Hog Island from the Swede Axel Wenner-Gren and gave it the more elegant name. Hartford dreamed of transforming the island into a resort of world-renowned luxury. He would make it the proximate Riviera, a tony playground for his rich friends, a place where money could mix with money 'neath the sun and the moon and the stars, and loll on the perfect beaches cozying up to the mild-mannered sea. He had no problem creating the right environment —he was a man of highly refined aesthetic sensibilities—but somehow his dream was crushed, and he knew who to blame: Resorts International.

Hartford's name showed up in some Resorts company reports—he had once sued them. A search through court records provided his address, though not his phone number, which turned out to be unlisted. I sent him a telegram—REQUEST SEE YOU RE: STORY ON RESORTS INTERNATIONAL—and he called the next day.

His voice was old and raspy. He said he would like to see me, but his lawyer wouldn't let him. He seemed anxious, an anxiety that may have grown out of obsession. He was a man who had sunk six years and perhaps hundreds of thousands of dollars into trying to recover an island and a fortune he said Resorts had stolen from him.

He called again and said his lawyer had agreed to let him talk, within limits. The lawyer would be present. Hartford lived on Beekman Place, one of Manhattan's most exclusive addresses, in a building that realtors call "prewar luxury high rise." His apartment was a duplex, its interior sedate, perhaps erring on the side of threadbare. There was a large terrace with an expensive view of the East River.

Hartford was a trim man, in his sixties, with an abundance of white hair. He introduced the lawyer, Michael Schoeman, who barely acknowledged the introduction. (Indeed, he wouldn't even disclose what firm he was with, though it was a cinch to find in a directory. A lot of Hartford's lawyers seemed less than 100 percent behind their client.) The small talk was brief. Hartford had a story to tell.

It began in 1959, when he purchased Hog Island, four hundred yards off the coast of Nassau, New Providence Island, the Bahamas. The only access then was by private boats or "bum boats," water taxis run by the natives. The land on Hog Island was largely undeveloped, but Hartford began to develop it.

In pursuit of his dream, he erected a luscious small hotel the color of strawberry ice cream, wrapped around a terrace and pretty little fish pools, surrounded by palm trees. He called it the Ocean Club. He hired Dick Wilson, renowned designer of golf courses, to plan the links, which eventually wove up and down and by the sea. He installed tennis courts. Tennis court number one was built to "championship dimensions" so it would suit his teacher, Pancho Gonzales. He imported, stone by stone from Europe, a cloister crafted in the twelfth century by Spanish monks, and reassembled it in what the brochures would call a Versailles garden of terraced design. Statues of obvious lineage were planted through the garden. He added a riding stable and a fine restaurant, the Cafe Martinique. He saw to every possible need his rich playmates might have. Paradise Island was a place of beauty, but it was not to be a place of prosperity. After the island opened—in January 1962, fanfared in the columns that dutifully reported on Hartford's gad-abouts—it promptly began losing money at the rate of a million dollars a year.

After a time, it seemed the only way it might make money would be to install a casino. Originally Hartford didn't want one any more than he wanted a bridge connecting Paradise Island to Nassau. His was to be an exclusive island. But eventually he began to think that seeing to it that his friends could gamble—as well as gambol—on Paradise Island was his only escape from financial ruin. So he set about getting the necessary approval, but the wrong way, or so it turned out.

In those days the Bahamas rulers were white, even though most of the population was black. The islands were a British colony whose Premier was Sir Roland Symonette. The man with the power, though, the real power, was Sir Stafford Sands, the minister of finance and tourism, a gentleman with a large say in who would have bestowed upon them "certificates of exemption." If you were lucky enough to get one, you were exempt from the laws of the Bahamas that forbade casinos. If you had one, you were in very exclusive company, because Stafford Sands was very stingy with them. Only three had been granted by the time, in the early sixties, that Hartford had his hankering.

But when Hartford tried to join that exclusive set, he made what turned out to be some big mistakes, all of which could be put under the general heading of irritating Stafford Sands.

The name Sir Stafford Sands is often preceded by adjectives such as "brilliant," "powerful," "ruthless." A lawyer by training, he bore no slight resemblance to Sidney Greenstreet in *The Maltese Falcon*—the fat man. One likes to think that in an office on Bay Street, Nassau, a fan turned silently over the head of Sir Stafford, who, one imagined, sat back in an antique wing chair, a white suit, neatly pressed and spotless, encompassing his largeness, a handkerchief occasionally pressed to his brow. He had a private law practice even while in government, and numbered among his clients some gambling interests from Freeport who paid him fees that were even fatter than his person. Thus did a poor civil servant make ends meet.

Huntington Hartford's first error was not hiring the right lawyer. He had lawyers all right, a battery of them, but not one of them was Stafford Sands. Hartford's lawyers advised him to make a political donation to the opposition party in Parliament, the black party, and he did so, fifteen thousand dollars. Bad politics, as far as Sands was concerned.

As if that wasn't enough, Hartford issued a press release upon which was typed the following treason:

"Babies are occasionally being born blind . . . and amoebic dysentery and tuberculosis are prevalent due to poor sanitation and overcrowding. If gambling would be permitted on Paradise Island, it goes without saying that there would be employment for thousands and I trust that my past record in giving employment will confirm the responsibility of my statement."

He promised to donate half the proceeds of the casino to the government for the welfare of the people of the islands.

No dice.

Stafford Sands, who once had penned glowing accolades to Hartford, praising him for the improvements he had made on Paradise Island, now dispatched a messenger to tell Hartford he would never be the recipient of a casino license. Sands didn't say why. The millionaire's grandiose political gestures to the wrong party no doubt played a part, but there are those who contend that Sands just didn't like Hartford, didn't like the way he conducted his private life, didn't like, as one report has it, his "sexual proclivities." At the time, explains one islander, those ran to "young girls with the bodies of boys." (Hartford was known to walk the beaches of Paradise Island and, upon setting his eyes on some tempting eighteen-year-old, strut toward her, stop by her beach towel and announce, "Hi! I'm Hunt Hartford. I own this island.")

For whatever reason, it had become plain to Hartford that he would have to find a partner if he wanted a casino. Eventually he found one, through an acquaintance in Miami. The partner was the Mary Carter Paint Company.

Hartford told me about the deal he made with Mary Carter

—how he lent them money to build a new hotel, and how a bridge from Nassau to Paradise Island was built, but with private, not company, funds, how Resorts eventually opened a casino, and how eventually Hartford's relationship with the company soured until finally the company forced him out of his share, pulling his holdings right out from under him. He sued, but they dragged the case out, he said, because he couldn't afford it and they knew it. So he was forced to settle.

The talk was interrupted at times by phone calls. Hartford would go off and speak in the hushed tones and coded messages one uses when one doesn't want others present to know what is being said. It was interrupted, too, when a young girl flitted in and was introduced as Hartford's wife. She looked about twenty-three. She sat quietly for a few moments, and though Hartford tried to include her in the conversation, she didn't seem particularly interested. When she left, Hartford led me to the second floor and there, in the hallway, pointed to an early map of Paradise Island.

"You see this golf course?" he asked. "I named it after the Arawac Indians, but Resorts changed it to Paradise Island Golf Course. The Arawacs were peaceful Indians, slain by the Carobs. That's what happens to peaceful people. You see this cloister? I imported it. Over here is the stable. The important thing to remember here is that out of an investment of thirty million, I came away with two million." He said his finances were not what they once had been, and that his greatest regret was that he had nothing to leave to his children.

For many weeks after the talk, he called. "*Mhisss* Mahon," he would say in a voice that begged for breath, "the important thing to remember here is that out of an investment of thirty million dollars, I got two million."

"*Mhisss* Mahon, I want to tell you about this new game I invented. I would like some publicity on it. It is a combination of Ping-Pong and paddle tennis. It is sure to be a success."

"*Mhisss* Mahon, I wonder if you can get a copy of this old magazine called *Sundance*. It had a story on Resorts International."

"*Mhisss* Mahon, this Paradise Island fiasco, it was one of the worst messes in American history. I didn't get a fucking thing!"

CHAPTER FIVE

I found an old clip from *The New York Times* which mentioned that in 1972, Martin Dardis, an investigator in the Miami state attorney's office, had looked into peculiar movements between the Bahamas and Florida. Specifically, between the Paradise Island Casino and the Key Biscayne Bank, which belonged to then-President Richard Nixon's friend Bebe Rebozo. There was speculation that the bank and the casino were laundering funds for the President. I called Dardis and, after several tries, reached him. He said that it was true he had looked into those activities in the early days of Watergate. In fact, he was instrumental in a lot of the early revelations about Watergate. He had scoffed at official explanations that it was a "routine burglary." Said Dardis, "A bunch of Cubans travel from Miami to Washington and break into Democratic headquarters in the middle of the night because they think they're going to find jewelry?"

Dardis said he was the one who found out about all of those hundred-thousand-dollar certificates of deposit floating in and out of Nixon's bank account at the Key Biscayne Bank. He had helped Woodward and Bernstein get the Watergate story, he claimed, and they made a million bucks out of it.

He said he had looked at money being filtered from Resorts International—whether it was legal or not, whether it was being skimmed out of the casino and laundered through Bebe's bank. There was a guy who worked for Resorts—Seymour Alter —whom a lot of people called Resorts' "bagman." "It was weird," said Dardis. "He had all this money going through his bank account, and he didn't make much more than twenty-five grand a year. But hundreds of thousands were traveling through bank accounts all over the place like money was going out of style."

Alter, said Dardis, would show up at the bank after hours and they would let him in. He would ask them to exchange little bills for big ones, and sometimes he'd putter around in a safe deposit box. Alter, said Dardis, "was like a nothing. He had a concession, a gift shop on Paradise Island. He sells it to three guys for three hundred or four hundred thousand dollars. It was worth maybe five or ten thousand bucks." (More amazing, it turned out, he didn't own the gift shop, and had sold only his *lease*.)

Alter used to work for Huntington Hartford, Dardis related. He ran his liquor store in New York, helped out with other things, then was Hartford's assistant on Paradise Island. Eventually, Hartford sued Resorts and its chairman, Crosby, "and how the hell Nixon, Abplanalp and Rebozo fit in, I don't know." Hartford's lawyers had contacted Dardis once and he went to New York to visit Hartford's home. "What a place. I was a Depression baby. It was very strange, being there. Lots of flunkies around, answering the telephone. And gophers. I didn't shop at the A and P."

As to Watergate, Dardis said he had tried to subpoena the Key Biscayne Bank records, but he got opposition all the way up to the White House. Ron Ziegler kept calling to protest, because Nixon had an account at that bank and the President's records were privileged. Dardis said, hell, he wasn't subpoenaing the President's records per se, he was subpoenaing the bank's. The bank even fought him on Alter's records. Finally the courts upheld Dardis, but with the proviso that he couldn't single out Nixon's records. So he threw in a few other names, like Amelia Earhart and the president of a big cola company. Eventually he got the records.

The records were weird, all right, Dardis said, and the bank was even weirder. A man named Franklin DeBoer was handling Nixon's trust accounts. Rebozo said he hired DeBoer out of the newspaper classifieds to be a trust officer. Dardis didn't believe him. Who hires a trust officer out of a newspaper, then gives him the account of the President of the United States? Franklin DeBoer turned out to have been convicted in New York on federal charges of mail and securities fraud. (And, as it happens, was a college roommate of Resorts' president, Jack Davis.)

Dardis had to get off the phone, but it was a real interesting cast of characters, he said. Why, once this guy Howard Cerny, who worked for Robert Vesco, flew down to Florida and offered Dardis a job with Vesco. Talked about flying around in corporate jets and stuff like that. "Made it sound real cushy."

Dardis said he had the files of depositions and checks and the certificates of deposit. He would be in New York the following week and would bring them with him. He would be staying at the St. Moritz Hotel and would call.

Only he didn't, and the hotel said there was no such person listed. His office said he was out of town. Days later, they said he was back but away from his desk and that he would return the call. He never did. So I went to Florida. I checked in that night at the Key Biscayne Hotel—it was somehow appropriate to the story, and quiet and off the beaten track of downtown Miami—and by nine the following morning, I was at the state attorney's office, asking to see Dardis. He was in court, the receptionist said, and I said I would wait.

The book *All the President's Men* makes mention of Dardis and describes that waiting room. Of the team of Woodward and Bernstein, it was Bernstein who was in contact with the investigator. Bernstein said that he had made an appointment to see Dardis but that Dardis had not kept it and, in fact, made Bernstein hang around all day. Bernstein said that while he was waiting, he had gone into the registrar's office of the state attorney and asked the clerk for copies of all subpoenas the state attorney's office had issued in the preceding months. He took note of the subpoenas issued in Dardis' name. Bernstein said that when Dardis finally showed up, he was a short man with a red face who dressed sloppily. Bernstein said that later Dardis tried to get him to help dig up dirt on a guy running for state attorney against Dardis' boss, Richard Gerstein.

I had a different experience. Dardis showed up not fifteen minutes after I sat down. He was a man of at least medium height, dapperly dressed, neat, with a raw Johnny Cash kind of voice. He ushered me immediately into his office, explained why he had not been in New York, pulled out a couple of boxes of files and let me go through the ones he thought would be of interest. I read while he moved in and out of the office and got on with his work. There was more of an education to be had from the office activity than from the files. Midmorning, for example, a woman was brought in accompanied by a small child. She had been arrested for trying to sell a baby across state lines. She was Cuban and spoke only Spanish. Working through a translator, Dardis told her in the strongest terms what would happen if she did it again. After she left, he explained that she had tried it many times and probably would once more.

He talked about Woodward and Bernstein, really upset about some of the things they said, like that he was dishonest and that Bernstein had been so clever looking up those subpoenas when he, Dardis, had had to spoon-feed him the information. Bernstein couldn't have gotten it otherwise. What really bothered him, though, was that Bernstein said he was a slob. That really hurt. Bernstein said he wore a blue blazer with frayed sleeves. "Anyone who knows me knows I don't dress like that," said Dardis. "I don't even own a blue blazer, and if I did, it wouldn't have frayed sleeves." He prided himself on being a good dresser, he added. Ask anyone. And Bernstein said he was short! Humph! If anybody was short, it was Carl Bernstein.

They wanted him to play himself in the movie version, he continued, but friends talked him out of it. He didn't really care, though. He said he didn't even care that Woodward and Bernstein made a fortune out of it.

Dardis said that after the courts upheld him about subpoenaing all those bank records, he got resistance to his investigation from other directions. The feds told him to lay off. He didn't know what he was getting into. So, he said, he did the only thing he could do—he tried to interest the press in the story. And just when he had decided to do so, along came Carl Bernstein, and the result was one of the biggest scandals in American history.

Dardis had other stories. He said that once he had gone to the Justice Department with information on organized-crime influence within the National Football League.

"That Justice Department was incredible," said Dardis. "You know how busy they were? They were standing around throwing darts at the wall, that's how busy they were. I went to this guy Hundley, William Hundley, the head of the organized-crime division. He didn't seem a bit interested in my story. Six months later, what happens? He leaves the Justice Department with this other guy Peloquin and they become lawyers for the National Football League."

Peloquin was a name I knew. Robert Peloquin was the president of Intertel—it stands for International Intelligence, the security subsidiary of Resorts International.

Dardis left again—he had to go over to Miami Beach—and I continued plowing through the files. The most interesting pieces concerned Sy Alter, the man who had worked for Hartford, then transferred allegiance to Resorts, the man they called the "bagman." Alter kept accounts at no fewer than six banks. One glance at his records would have given the average accountant apoplexy. As Dardis had said, Alter, who later would testify that he drew a $25,000 salary from Resorts and once had an equal pension from Hartford (which was no longer forthcoming), dealt actively in checks of amounts like $100,000 and $225,000.

The Dardis office had called Richard Stearns, a Key Biscayne Bank employee, to testify. (The bank recommended a lawyer to him, the same man who represented John Ehrlichman.) It was Stearns who told of Alter's after-hours visits to the bank to change ten- and twenty-dollar bills into larger ones. Stearns drew no conclusions from that. He wasn't paid to question customers' activities. Besides, he said, the after-hours visits weren't that unusual. Lots of Bebe's friends did it.

Stearns was asked who Alter was, and he replied that he was a good buddy of Bebe Rebozo's. On perhaps five occasions, the bank lent Alter large sums of money. Stearns thought one of the loans was for $70,000 or $80,000 and that Alter had used the money to buy stock in Resorts International. Also, when Stearns first joined the bank in 1968, Alter had a nice little savings account there, maybe as much as $50,000.

Then there was the testimony from Alter. How had a man of his moderate means, the questioner wondered, managed to accumulate hundreds of thousands of dollars? Well, came the reply, he had a gift shop in the arcade at the Britannia Beach Hotel on Paradise Island, and he sold it (to General Bahamian Companies, a Robert Vesco outfit) for $315,000. He said the reason he had so many accounts at different banks was that he thought it was the safe thing to do. He didn't want to lose his money by putting it all in one place. He didn't know you could buy certificates of deposit in denominations of $100,000 and get more interest. He was afraid that such large sums would not be covered by federal insurance, so he spread things out.

What of those after-hours visits? investigators wondered. His answer: The Bahamian government had forbidden the transport of U.S. dollars out of the country, so he had snuck his out, having instructed the personnel in the gift shop to squirrel them away. Eventually, he transported the money to Florida.

Dardis was not satisfied nor, it turned out, was just about any other investigator who looked into the transactions. Why was the lease to a small gift shop hawking T-shirts, cigarettes, magazines and perfume worth more than $300,000? (What Alter paid for the shop was not known, except that he had borrowed $30,000 for "opening expenses.") Why would a bank lend a man double his income—and more? Why were all of those bills from the gift shop in tens and twenties? That sounded more like casino money than gift-shop bills. Gift shops should have lots of ones and fives. Why put all of that money in the Key Biscayne Bank? Said Dardis, "Alter said it was handy. It wasn't handy. It's way the hell out of the way."

But sitting in Dardis' office turning page after page, canceled check after canceled check, I found it hard to draw conclusions. Guesses yes, conclusions no.

I later came across a similar story about Seymour Alter in 1975 testimony by an IRS informant, Norm Casper, to a U.S. House of Representatives subcommittee investigating the IRS. In recounting the events of the fall of 1972, Casper told the congressmen about a two-dollar toll on the bridge between Nassau and Paradise Island—the bridge owned mostly by Resorts' chairman, James Crosby. When someone pays the toll with Bahamian dollars, he said, "it goes into a regular

Bahamian bank account for regular accounting." But when an American dollar goes in, it gets thrown back into a box, a kind of safe in the bridge office, and not a very secure safe at that, he said.

One day, according to Casper, a man who had just taken over as assistant director of security came to the office. He said, "Wait a minute, this is vulnerable because we can get held up." There was more than $200,000 in that safe. He put the money in the back of his car and drove around with it for a couple of days, wondering what to do. Finally he took it over to the casino, and there it was placed in a vault, where it stayed until one day, Casper told the committee, "the money left. It just wasn't there because normally he [the guard] would see it as he made his security rounds."

The same day that the money disappeared, said Casper, a gentleman named Sy Alter, who is a close friend of Bebe Rebozo's, left the island. He boarded a Chalk's airplane (Chalk's is, as of 1974, the airline owned by Resorts International) and flew to Miami. Once in Miami, he went to the Jockey Club, a condominium where Resorts keeps apartments.

At the same time, Frank Lichtenburg, the captain of the Resorts International yacht *Orca,* was in Miami for some boat repairs. He got a call from the Dinner Key Marina area to get the boat up to the Jockey Club "real fast, posthaste," to pick up Sy Alter. Frank went up to the Jockey Club with the boat, and waiting for him, said Casper, was Sy, carrying a briefcase. Alter said to the captain, "I am going to see the man. Get me over to the Key Biscayne Yacht Club as fast as you can get me there." He was quite nervous, related Casper.

"They got there and Bebe drove on the dock. He was driving a black Lincoln Continental. Sy climbed in the car real quick, but prior to that Sy said, 'I am going to see the man.' "

Casper continued: "Nixon was in town at the time. He was in the house on Bay Lane. They headed for either Bebe's house or Nixon's house. Sy Alter, according to published newspaper reports here some time back, had accounts at the Key Biscayne Bank. He had been acquainted with Bebe Rebozo for years. Sy has been known as the bagman for Resorts International for quite some time. These are not my terms but terms used in media reporting. Everything that I can find at the Resorts International or the Paradise Island complex tended to bear that out, that he was known as the bagman. He was the man who transferred money for Resorts International, for what purpose who knows, via Chalk Airways."

For what purpose, who knows? The subcommittee never found out, but its members were certainly intrigued. Who *was* Sy Alter? they wondered. The answer was easy: one more enigma in the story of Resorts International.

CHAPTER SIX

In a book called *Vesco: The Looting of IOS,* * stated as fact was something that others had only guessed at. Resorts International had once negotiated to sell Paradise Island to Robert Vesco, the wealthy mutual-fund "czar" turned fugitive. Everyone knew that. What everyone only conjectured was what the book's author, Robert Hutchison, also reported as follows:

Cerny and Straub [Vesco men] were particularly interested in the skimming procedures whereby, it was discovered, millions of dollars were diverted from the cash receipts allegedly without appearing in the books of Paradise Enterprises Limited, the operator of the casino. The skimming implied the continued presence of a Mafia credit man inside the casino. According to one of Vesco's Super Group lawyers, the system centered upon the acceptance of IOU notes from known creditworthy players. The IOUs would not be cleared through the casino's accounting department but would be placed aside and taken to Miami, where they were discounted for cash with a Mob-connected collection agency or bank.

---

*New York: Praeger, 1974.

Hutchison was living in Switzerland. When I phoned him there and asked if he remembered the quote, he laughed. He hadn't been allowed to forget it. He said that his sources were people who were very close to the situation. But, he added, Resorts International had threatened to sue him and Praeger, the publisher, unless it retracted the lines on the skim. Praeger consulted with Hutchison, who said he stood by the story, but he had to admit he could not guarantee his sources would stand up and testify in court if it came to that. So Praeger wrote a letter of retraction to Resorts, and the publisher agreed to delete the offending paragraph from all future editions of the book. The funny thing was, the edition I read was the paperback, published long after Praeger had written the retraction, and the statement was still there, clear as ink. Somehow it had slipped by.

Nor was *Vesco* the only controversy-engendering tale of Resorts International. *Rolling Stone* magazine is being sued for libel by Resorts because in the May 20, 1976, issue, the magazine claimed that Resorts, in its earlier incarnation as Mary Carter Paint, was a CIA front set up by former New York district attorney and governor Thomas Dewey and Allen Dulles, first chief of the CIA, to launder funds to support counterinsurgency groups in Latin America. (I have had a Freedom of Information request in with the CIA for two years. They admit they have files on Mary Carter/Resorts, but to date have found excuses not to produce them.) Resorts waited a couple of months before it sued—until the story was picked up by the then-all-important Atlantic City press. Some observers guessed that Resorts was acting only to save face, and that it would let the suit die a quiet death. At this writing, almost four years later, it looks like that is a possibility.

A young Midwestern lawyer told me that "there have been red flags in Resorts International's files at the SEC ever since it was Mary Carter Paint." The problem on following up on whether that was still true is that the SEC is not keen, in general, on talking about what they are investigating to the members of the press—that is, members of the press to whom they are not in the habit of leaking stories.

I called Stanley Sporkin, head of enforcement at the SEC, who probably has more clout than anyone else in the agency except the commissioners (and even that is debatable). When I reached Sporkin, he said that it was a matter of record that the SEC had often investigated Resorts and their associates, usually in regard to stock manipulation. But he said he wasn't allowed to comment on whether there was a pending investigation. And, he added, *Barron's* was always the first to gripe when the SEC revealed investigations. He said if past cases were closed, I could go through them, but I would have to use the Freedom of Information process. If the cases were not closed, I couldn't look at them. Anyway, he said, "you can't investigate people just because you think they're not nice guys." He added that if I wanted to know about Resorts International, I should ask Stu Allen, and that was the end of the conversation.

Stu Allen was an SEC lawyer, and he said he had never had anything to do with any investigation of Resorts International. I asked him why someone in the SEC would mention his name. "I guess because I used to work there," he said. It turned out he had worked for Intertel. He had left the SEC to go there, but had quickly returned to the SEC. Why? I wanted to know. He said he didn't want to talk about it. Why not? He wouldn't say that, either.

I asked him, "If you thought the company was spanking clean and honest, a model corporate citizen, would you talk about it?"

"Yes, I would."
"But you won't talk about it?"
"No."

Another government investigator was more forthcoming. When I called him, he said, in effect, Well, I really don't know much about it, and if I did, why should I tell you? Still, he agreed to see me in Washington and he ended up being very helpful. He said Resorts had been investigated since the sixties by the Justice Department because it was thought somewhat strange that this little paint company was getting into the casino business.

Resorts was also investigated because the SEC thought it was unusual that a casino company was trying to buy a major airline, Pan Am. The investigator described later haggles the SEC had with Resorts over writing down the value on its books of the Pan Am stock, which the agency said wasn't worth what Resorts claimed. The commission won that one. And throughout the years, Resorts had been investigated because its stock was always doing crazy things, going up and down, wildly sometimes.

Then he rummaged through some files and came up with two wonderful sheets of paper. They were blueprints of the funding of Mary Carter's beginnings on Paradise Island— names of all of the people and banks that had lent it money —and of all of the money behind the mysterious bridge connecting Paradise Island and Nassau. Neither of these had been detailed before in print, as far as I knew. The bridge had always been under a cloud of secrecy, since James Crosby refused to say who owned it with him. There was constant speculation that the silent partners were Nixon and Rebozo. Those names were not on the sheet, but something called Cosmos Bahamian, Limited, was. The man said that Cosmos was a Swiss bank, a front for a group of investors. He said he couldn't remember offhand who the investors were, but he would scrounge around and see what he could come up with. He never did come up with it, but much later I did find out, and one of the names was startlingly familiar.

An executive of Resorts International once said, If you want to know how clean we are, just ask the Watergate investigators. They were all over Paradise Island and left satisfied that nothing was wrong.

I called a man who had been an important fixture in the Senate Watergate hearings, and asked him if he remembered the name Resorts International.

"Sure," he said, "we received allegations regarding the possibility that Rebozo had received cash from them. We sent a guy down to Paradise Island, but he came back without much success. He was not a lawyer. We stopped the investigation because we ran out of time and we ran out of money. Nothing was ever solved to my satisfaction. It was definitely unfinished."

CHAPTER SEVEN

The weeks wore on. The story was like some exotic creature that kept growing new limbs. Every time it seemed to be contained, someone would say something that would set it off in a whole new direction that had to be tracked down.

For example, someone said that the brother of an organized-crime figure was a cashier at the Paradise Island Casino and, while there, had been given $50,000 by a Robert Vesco bank. No one could figure out why—and I never did either.

Someone else said Paradise Island seemed almost to be a haven for criminals or at least people who were wanted for questioning. For example, a man named Frank Mace, who was wanted for questioning by the SEC, stayed at the Ocean Club instead of facing the music. A couple of people wanted for insurance fraud in England were living on the island, as was Frank Lloyd, former head of New York's Marlborough Galleries, who was under indictment in New York for tampering with evidence in the Rothko art case. These people all did turn out to have lived on the island from time to time.

A source who used to work in Nassau said that Resorts once had a peculiar bank, the Vortec Bank, set up in a room in a Vesco building in Nassau. The bank consisted of a Telex ma-

chine and two telephones on the floor, and it was visited occasionally by Columbus O'Donnell, a nephew of Huntington
Hartford's who continued to work for Resorts after his uncle
was gone. Resorts eventually admitted the existence of this
"bank."

A Justice Department official explained the difficulties of
trying to find out what was going on with a company that had
the bulk of its operations in the Bahamas—they could hide
almost anything.

A librarian from Atlantic City said the ladies' room at the
Marlborough-Blenheim Hotel had always been tacky. She had
stayed in a hotel in Madrid for twenty-five dollars a night that
was a lot more luxurious. And, by the way, there were an awful
lot of charges that Resorts International was too close to the
legislators writing the casino laws. Whatever the casinos
wanted, she said, they eventually got. The state was pragmatic
—they liked the kind of money spread around by people like
Bally, a slot-machine manufacturer that planned to open a
casino. There was a furor over state legislators taking trips to
far-off gambling meccas, and a continued debate over who had
paid for what on those journeys and who should or should not
have.

Repeated calls I made to Huntington Hartford's former law
firm, Stroock and Stroock and Lavan, the one that unsuccessfully represented him in his lawsuit against Resorts, went un-
returned. So did calls to Russell Weiss, chairman of the Bank
of Commerce, which Hartford alleged had been instrumental
in his losing his share of the island. Weiss was a close friend
and long-time business associate of Resorts' chairman, James
Crosby.

A couple of Nevada enforcement people, when asked if the
New Jersey law was tougher than theirs, said they hadn't read
it, but they wished they were making as much money as all the
enforcement people they heard about in New Jersey.

More calls, more questions, more dead ends. There came a point when it was time to go back to the company and talk to management.

The first Resorts official I spoke to was Robert Peloquin, head of Intertel, the Resorts security organization. He had formerly been with the Justice Department, where his track record had been, by many accounts, a good one. Peloquin was the chief of the first Organized Crime Strike Force at Justice and a senior attorney in the organized-crime and racketeering section. In the late sixties, while at Justice, he investigated gambling in the Bahamas, including Mary Carter's entry into casinos. As a result of that investigation, he wrote a memo which concluded that "the atmosphere seems ripe for a Lansky skim."

Shortly after, Peloquin left Justice and, with fellow department lawyer William Hundley, became counsel to the National Football League. (It should be remembered that Martin Dardis, the Florida investigator, said he had tried unsuccessfully to interest Hundley in negative information about the NFL.) Later the two men opened a law firm, and among their clients, in addition to the league, was Mary Carter Paint. Eventually, with $2 million from Resorts International, Peloquin formed Intertel, which would be a subsidiary of Resorts.

When I tried to reach Peloquin by phone, I found him at home. A Wall Street executive's voice was once described as "a claw coming through the wires," a line I remembered when I heard Peloquin's voice.

I told him who I was and, after some preliminaries, made the mistake of asking him about the "Lansky skim" memo. He wouldn't admit he had written it. "I'd have to see it," he snapped. His tone was very nasty. He went off into a tirade about how he was sick of reporters crawling all over the place and how I'd "just better watch it. We already have one lawsuit going. We wouldn't mind another." He said he didn't respond to questions by phone, then he hung up.

A few days later I called Peloquin from the National Airport outside Washington and asked to see him. What I got on the other end must have been his Dr. Jeckyll side. Sweet, almost affable. Nice. I was very suspicious. *Do* come over, he said.

At his office he was still friendly and said he was so sorry about the way he had behaved the other day. He was cranky because he was sick, he said, and besides, ever since Resorts had hit Atlantic City, reporters had been around like a "swarm of bees." No matter what you told them, they wrote whatever they felt like writing, never got even half the story right.

But we sat down and he went through it once more. He answered all the questions, and when sensitive issues were brought up, he laughed heartily and explained how this particular story had gotten started, and how it wasn't true, and how that particular reporter had finally had to admit he had been wrong and write a retraction.

We got to chatting about other things and somehow established that he had grown up next door to my college roommate's family in Massachusetts. There were other inconsequentialities; then it was over. While waiting for the elevator in the reception room, I smiled at the young woman behind the desk and murmured something like "Pretty day, isn't it?" She glared defiantly. "Mr. Peloquin is a *wonderful* man," she said. "We love working for him."

"Yes," I said, and got in the elevator, reminding myself that nice means nothing. He may have been perfectly wonderful, but on the other hand, some of the greatest crooks of all times could charm the pants off penguins.

I didn't see him or speak to him again for a year and a half. That was on the Boardwalk, only weeks before five commissioners would decide whether or not to give Resorts a permanent license to operate in Atlantic City. I was walking out of the hearing building with a friend, Bruce Hallett, then with the New York *Daily News,* when a voice called out from behind: "Are you going to be gentle with us, Miss Mahon?" It was Peloquin, sporting a broad, ironic grin. Bruce said, "That's a smile that comes from being smug. They know they've won."

The phone call I saved for last was to James M. Crosby, the chairman of Resorts International and the scion of the founding family. I was fascinated by his picture in the annual report. He looked like James Bond, handsome in a cold kind of way, with black hair, black eyes, a hard jaw. In real life he resembles James Bond as much as Frank Perdue does. In real life he is on the small side, frail, pale, stooped, sickly. His speech is punctuated more often with coughs than commas.

He answered my questions, but sometimes he gave different answers than Peloquin to the same questions. Sometimes they disagreed on things one was apt to forget, like dates. But there were contradictions, too, on more important issues, like what Sy Alter had been doing transporting money to Key Biscayne and whether Intertel warned Crosby off dealing with Robert Vesco when Vesco was about to be indicted.

Then I asked the question that begged for an answer: Who were the secret investors in the Paradise Island Bridge? Crosby wouldn't say, except that they were "people of substance, but not notoriety." And not, he said, Nixon and Rebozo.

Following that interview, I sat down and spread all the notes and all the documents in front of me, then began to write what eventually became a two-part story, published in *Barron's* in September and October 1977.

PART TWO

THE
STORY

CHAPTER EIGHT

The story begins with a family named Crosby. There was a father, James F. Crosby, who produced a diverse array of sons. One is a real estate man and franchise owner, another a plastic surgeon. The third is a convicted felon and sometime jailbird, and the last, the one this story concerns, a former stockbroker who ended up running a casino company.

The father was a lawyer and a sometime public servant. He was a deputy attorney general in the Woodrow Wilson administration and an attorney general in the state of Connecticut. He was also a businessman of no minor means. The family business was out of Wisconsin, though the Crosbys made their homes mostly on the East Coast. The business was started from Schaefer Manufacturing Company, a foundry and manufacturing concern. It was acquired by John Crosby in 1955 and the name was later changed to Crosby-Miller.

In 1958 Crosby-Miller authorized a 25 percent increase in its number of shares and sold the new shares to a group which was headed by Thomas E. Dewey, once governor of New York and former crime-busting New York district attorney, and which included Lowell Thomas, author and "personality." The Crosby and Dewey groups together quickly bought another company, Mary Carter Paint. (The Dewey group did not stay associated with the company for long, and the Dewey family today protests that it was out of Mary Carter long before it went into the casino business.)

One of the four Crosby sons takes credit for the acquisition of Mary Carter Paint. He is James Morris Crosby, born in Great Neck, Long Island, in 1928. His early education was in Washington, D.C., after which he attended three prep schools —his father, he said, had novel ideas about education—before graduating from Lawrenceville, in New Jersey, and later Georgetown University. Upon graduation, he put in a year at International Paint Company, then moved to Harris Upham, a New York brokerage firm. There Crosby worked initially as a stockbroker, buying and selling securities, then later became involved in mergers and acquisitions.

Jim Crosby's father wasn't much taken by the stockbrokering business. He thought his son should do something that provided more security, perhaps be a lawyer, but Jim liked his job well enough to stay there for eight years. His next stop was a stint with a D.C. financier named Gustave Ring, for whom he evaluated acquisition proposals. That lasted a short, but valuable, four months. Out of it came Crosby's involvement with two companies that were to figure prominently in his future: Unexcelled Chemical Corporation and Mary Carter Paint Company.

Ring owned some stock in Unexcelled, and Crosby had brushed up against the company while a stockbroker. In the late fifties, Crosby was involved in a successful proxy fight— a dump-management campaign—and eventually took over as president of Unexcelled. The amazing thing, he recalled later, was that he always thought that Mary Carter Paint was a perfect acquisition for Unexcelled, but that had gotten lost in the proxy shuffle. Then, as noted, his family and the Dewey group decided to buy Mary Carter, and the same day that the family deal went through, in early December of 1958, young Crosby was installed as the head of Unexcelled. He quickly dismissed plans for a merger of the two companies—it now seemed a conflict of interest, since his family was involved in both.

In the beginning, young Crosby devoted most of his energies to running Unexcelled (while he was simultaneously chairman of Mary Carter Paint), an eclectic company that numbered among its businesses an ornamental-paint manufacturer, a fireworks producer, a meat-packing and leasing concern. The stock was often as highflying as the fireworks. There was lots to excite investors. In 1960, for example, Unexcelled said it had perfected a fantastic invention, the Skyjector, a mammoth machine that could project advertisements on the sides of mountains and clouds. On its first exhibition run, it projected pictures of Richard Nixon, Brigitte Bardot and a Pepsi bottle cap on the side of a building next to a vacant lot in Manhattan's West Side. The plan was to charge advertisers $3,000 for a forty-five-minute display.

A blitzkrieg of publicity attended the introduction of the thing, but it died a less publicized death. If it had lived, it might have raised some interesting environmental questions, like whether moonlight strollers should be forced to look at Richard Nixon's bid for the presidency on the side of a fluffy cloud or if nighttime skiers should be made to slide down the face of a Coors beer can.

By 1967 Crosby would have extricated himself from Unexcelled Chemical, though he would always retain a sort of incestuous relationship to it. Some of its directors would be Mary Carter's directors. Its lawyers would be Mary Carter's lawyers. And later on, Unexcelled would change its name to Twin Fair, and Twin Fair, among other acquisitions, would pick up Mary Carter Paint, which by that time would have been dumped by the Crosbys too.

CHAPTER NINE

The year 1960 is probably as good a place as any to begin to unravel the tangled ball of twine that is Mary Carter Paint–Resorts International. By 1960 the important corporate characters of Mary Carter Paint were in place. The executive suite housed two men who would figure inextricably in everything that Mary Carter was to become. One was James Crosby, the other was Irving George "Jack" Davis. Westchester, New York–born, Davis attended Williams College and, after a tour in the Air Force, went on to Harvard Business School. He was well tailored into his expensive blazers and looked like he might be at home in some fast-track Wall Street investment banking firm or at some glamorous conglomerate, but not at a little paint company.

Also in place in the early sixties was a board of directors, comprised mostly of management and family. There were three of the four Crosby brothers—the black sheep, Francis Peter, was excluded—and their Murphy cousins. Charles Murphy was a lawyer and counsel to Mary Carter. Cousin Henry was a Trenton, New Jersey, funeral home director who was married to a Crosby sister, Elaine. The Murphys and the Crosbys had met in childhood summers in the shore town of Spring

Lake, New Jersey. There was, on the board, another lawyer from Charlie's law firm and a long-time business associate, John Miller. It was a cozy little group that gathered for those board of directors meetings. No outsiders need apply. That closeness was exhibited, too, in the way the stock was set up when Mary Carter eventually went public. There were A and B shares. There were many more A than B, but each B controlled a hundred votes while each A controlled only one. Most of the B was in the hands of management. As long as they retain that system, which they have to date, they will never be able to trade on the New York Stock Exchange, but must trade instead on the much less prestigious American Stock Exchange, or AMEX.

In the early sixties, most of Mary Carter's dabblings were confined to the primary business, paints, and early on it became apparent that the new regime at Mary Carter had inherited some problems with the law from its predecessors.

Mary Carter had a slogan: Buy one, get one free (meaning cans of paint). But the Federal Trade Commission argued that they didn't quite mean it. The FTC said that two cans of paint were being offered for the price of two cans of paint. Resorts said it was perfectly legitimate advertising. The Federal Trade Commission didn't grasp the subtlety and thought it was downright misleading. They told Mary Carter to cease and desist.

Crosby was having none of it. He marched over to the New York law offices of politically power-packed Dewey Ballantine and explained his dilemma to Thomas Dewey. Dewey said that he certainly thought Mary Carter Paint had the meritorious side of the case and took Crosby over to see Judge David Peck at another Wall Street law firm, Sullivan and Cromwell. Judge Peck agreed. Then some courts did, some didn't, and the argument found its way all the way up to the Supreme Court, where the high judges begged to differ with Crosby, Dewey and Peck. That was the end of "Buy one, get one free." All Mary Carter had to show for it was a fortune in legal fees. The Supreme Court didn't hand down its decision until 1965, and in those intervening years a lot had happened to change the face of Mary Carter Paint.

In 1960, at a tennis club in Miami, Crosby had met a lawyer, Richard Olsen. In the course of conversation, Crosby told Olsen that his company, Mary Carter, was looking for diversification and would like to know if Olsen came across anything suitable. Two years later, Olsen had a prospect involving acquaintances of his on Grand Bahama Island, the Bahamas. They owned a land development company, Bahamas Developers, that wasn't doing too well, and they were strapped for the first mortgage payment. Mary Carter Paint stepped in and bought the company and its land on Grand Bahama. The deal was not particularly important in company history, but Olsen's next idea would be.

CHAPTER TEN

Events taking place in the Bahamas and Cuba as far back as the 1950s set the stage for the future of casinos—and Mary Carter Paint—in the islands. In 1959 a bearded fanatic took control of Cuba, a field where organized crime had fruitfully tilled not sugar cane but casinos. Fidel Castro put an end to those capitalistic centers of depravity and, at the same time, to a source of billions of dollars to the mob.

Organized crime looked elsewhere for prosperity, and simple logic led it to train its sights mere miles northeastward, to the Bahamas. This happy little sprinkling of islands boasted many of the same ingredients as Cuba: blue skies, calm waters, gentle breezes—and an easily corrupted government. Racketeer Meyer Lansky had lost the powerful services of his good friend, deposed Cuban leader Fulgencio Batista, but perhaps he could find no less an ally in the most powerful man in the Bahamas, Sir Stafford Sands, the minister of finance and tourism.

Lansky visited Sands in 1960, armed with a proposition which had to do with casinos: he wanted to bring them to the Bahamas. The islands might thus enjoy all of the attendant benefits, like increased tourism and higher revenues—and Sands stood to gain too. Lansky offered him $2 million worth of "legal fees." Sands later told a Royal Commission of Inquiry that he booted the brazen buccaneer out. Events would seem to indicate otherwise.

The law of the Bahamas forbade gambling casinos and, until the 1960s, only two exceptions were made. A couple of small "clubs" were allowed to operate casinos at high tourist season. One was on Cat Cay; the other, the Bahamian Club, was on the outskirts of Nassau. Sentiment in the Bahamas did not favor the addition of more casinos, but the low odds did not deter Stafford Sands from trying. As early as 1945, when Sands was thirty-two and already a powerful political figure, he had tried to force approval for a twenty-five-year monopoly on casinos for a syndicate of which he was a member. The following year, after many doubts had been voiced in the all-important Executive Council about the prospect of more casinos, Sands finally withdrew from the syndicate because his participation, he realized, "might cause embarrassment to government." Despite his withdrawal, the petition was rejected.

It would be many years before Sands was successful, and when he was, it would be in the name of two men, Wallace Groves and Louis Chesler. Wallace Groves was an American, a convicted stock swindler on one hand, and on the other the visionary whose grand plan was Freeport, an international trading port in the Bahamas. Louis Chesler was a real estate man, originally from Canada, who was active in the formation of Florida's General Development Corporation, one of the major U.S. land developers. He was a man of enormous physical proportions, weighing in at over three hundred pounds. The names Groves and Chesler both spelled m-o-b in law enforcement circles.

Groves got to the island first. After his conviction in the United States, he had gone to the Bahamas to lick his wounds. He arrived in the forties and started a lumber business called Abaco. The way legend later had it, he practically chopped down the whole island himself. Before long, Groves started to consider the future possibilities of Grand Bahama Island. His original notion was the placement on the island of a port in which all imports and exports would be duty-free. He discussed the idea with his friend Stafford Sands, then a member of the House of Assembly. Sands was not enthusiastic: he didn't see how the government could make any money out of the deal.

In 1953 Groves came up with an amended plan. Consumer goods would be subject to duties, but manufacturing and building materials needed for development would not. All Bahamian-made goods would be free of export duties. That idea took. Sands drafted the Hawksbill Creek Act, a contract between the governor in council and the Port Authority, a company set up by Groves and vested with quasi-governmental powers. Under the agreement, signed in 1955, the government agreed to grant purchase of Crown land to the Port Authority if the latter would dredge a deep-water harbor and construct a wharf to accommodate cargo boats. More land was "granted" for the purpose of industrial development.

By 1960, despite all the fancy plans, not much had happened. Only one big project had been undertaken. The problem was, companies feared that employees would refuse to live on Grand Bahama Island. There was nothing to do there and no schools or homes. So, starting in 1960, the Port Authority beefed up its effort to lure tourist and residential development. The Hawksbill Creek Act was changed to allow some land slated for industrial development to be dedicated, instead, to residential. The Port Authority agreed to build at least one first-class hotel.

Enter Louis Chesler in 1961. It was thought that his experience in land development would prove invaluable. Sands called him the most outstanding real estate salesman he had ever known. A fellow executive called him a "high promotion individual." He was flamboyant, a compulsive gambler, usually on the losing side. Sands introduced Chesler both to the concept of Grand Bahama and to Groves. Chesler and Groves formed the Grand Bahama Development Company with one hundred acres of Port Authority land. In return for the land, the Port Authority got half ownership in the development company.

Despite Chesler's reputed real estate savvy, by 1962 he and Groves felt compelled to seek the guidance of Sir Stafford in his capacity as friend and minister. Their project was still not successful, and they blamed their failures on the lack of first-class hotels and tourist facilities. But they had a solution, they told Sands: casinos. The minister needed little persuasion. In March 1963, Sands made a proposal to the Executive Council, of which he was a member, for the granting of a certificate of exemption to a new Groves-Chesler company, Bahamas Amusements. Council meetings were conducted in secret because of the known hostility among a large and influential section of the population to more casinos.

Groves and Chesler didn't need the public; they knew the power of Sands. They were so certain that the minister would come through for them that they started construction on the Lucayan Beach Hotel and its Monte Carlo Casino long before the vote came up. But they took no chances on leaks that might ruin the vote. In the architectural plans, the huge space by the front door was labeled "handball courts."

Six months before the license was granted, according to Louis Chesler's later statement to the Justice Department, a meeting was held at the Fontainebleau Hotel in Miami Beach to discuss the casino. Among those attending were Chesler, Michael "Trigger Mike" Coppola, Charles "Charlie the Blade" Turine, Jake Lansky and his brother Meyer, Dino Cellini, Frank Ritter, Max Courtney and Charles Brudner. The last three were under indictment in New York for racketeering and gambling violations. (Two later returned and were convicted. The third, Brudner, did not stand trial due to illness.)

Meyer Lansky himself met with the hotel-casino architect on at least three occasions to discuss the "handball courts." When the equipment, including roulette and crap tables, blackjack tables and slot machines arrived, Lansky directed its placement.

On April 1, eleven days after Sands presented the application for the certificate and used his powers of persuasion on his fellow councilmen, the exemption was granted. In return for his "legal services" to the petitioners, according to a royal commission report, Sands was paid more than $500,000 and possibly over a million; the commission could never determine the amount.

Within a week of the vote, five of the nine men in the Executive Council had signed consultancy agreements with Groves and Chesler. For example, Dr. Raymond Sawyer, a dentist, agreed to consult for five years on medical and dental facilities on Grand Bahama Island. The maximum time required per year would be one hundred hours. His retainer was one of the lower ones in the group—about $6,000 a year. He later admitted he had never rendered any services because nobody ever asked him to. That was the case with most of the consultants. When the dentist was later asked by an investigating committee if the amount involved didn't seem excessive for the work required, he said of course not. As a dentist in the Bahamas, he needed at least $75,000 to $100,000 a year to "get by."

After the opening of the Freeport Monte Carlo Casino, Lansky faded into the background—he lived in Miami Beach—and left behind Dino Cellini, his brother Eddie Cellini and the three fugitives from New York—Ritter, Courtney and Brudner—who, the royal commission later conjectured, still served their "sinister masters across the water." Also after the opening, Dan "Dusty" Peters, the self-described chief of public relations at the Lucayan Beach

Hotel, traveled weekly to Miami with a satchel and went directly to the cardroom of the Fontainebleau Hotel, where Meyer Lansky waited. American authorities guessed that Peters was a courier for Lansky, bringing him the weekly skim from the casino.

CHAPTER ELEVEN

One of the more interested observers of the doings on Grand Bahama was Huntington Hartford, who had been ensconced on Paradise Island since 1959. Hartford felt cheated, felt that the other island had been given a competitive edge, because his island, casino-less, was a financial flop.

At that time, Hartford had an employee, Seymour Alter. Alter was a burly, smashed-nose man who often wore pink-tinted glasses. He could have been Central Casting for the extra in the gangster movie—the heavy, the thug. He looked, Robert Peloquin once said, "as if somebody had stepped on his face." Peloquin added, "But he's a real sweet guy."

Alter was an all-round man for Hartford: part handyman, part executive assistant, part official greeter, part fixer. He had been with Hartford for decades, long enough to manage his liquor store (they got into troubles on licensing with that one, and Alter tried to bribe a judge to fix it), to help out in his modeling agency (a short-lived venture Hartford started to meet girls) and to try to bring prosperity to other ill-fated ventures.

In the early sixties, Hartford was grappling with his newest problem acquisition—his island. Alter remembers that in the beginning of Paradise Island, Hartford would call meetings at midnight, seeking advice as night staggered into day, wondering what to build and where to build it. The island Hartford had so carefully planned was not a success because Sir Stafford Sands repeatedly refused his requests for a casino license. Nothing—not lawyers, not promises, not contributions—could change the minister's mind. Hartford had even tried to sway Sands by finding some influential allies. In the fall of 1962, Hartford had a meeting at the Fontainebleau Hotel in Miami with Sam Golub and Alvin Malnik. Golub was a Florida businessman who had the reputation of having good connections in the Bahamas, especially with Sands. Malnik was a Miami Beach lawyer who has been alleged to be a "front" for Meyer Lansky. Hartford signed a contract with the two men in which he agreed to pay them a substantial fee if they could get him a gaming license. When the contract expired sixty days later, they had not been successful.

The following year, after the casino license was granted to Grand Bahama, and after Sands dispatched a messenger to inform Hartford that in order to get a license he must get a suitable partner, Hartford became resigned to the idea, realizing that to follow other than the irascible fat man's dictum would spell financial ruin. So he put out some feelers and prevailed upon Sy Alter to help him find a buyer. There were a few nibbles, but nothing came of them. Alter claims to have been approached by lawyer Alvin Malnik, the same Miami contact Hartford had contracted with. Alter later told investigators that Malnik said he had a potential buyer for the island and took him to a Miami restaurant for a meeting with Meyer Lansky. Alter said he told them Hartford would certainly not be interested in dealing with Lansky. Malnik denies the story.

The year 1964 brought hope in the person of Richard Olsen, the Miami lawyer who previously helped Mary Carter buy the Grand Bahama land. Acquainted with Olsen from a Miami tennis club (the same club at which Olsen had met Crosby), Hartford told him his troubles and Olsen told Mary Carter chairman Crosby that this might be a new opportunity for his company. Crosby toured Paradise Island, which by then had been closed down, and said he was interested.

In February 1965, Crosby and lawyer Charlie Murphy met with Hartford at his Beekman Place apartment. Hartford insisted the visitors take a handwriting test. He felt he could tell a lot about a man's character that way. They had to write, Crosby later remembered, "a buggy in the garage," and they were supposed to write it twice. Murphy passed the test, but Crosby flunked. The meeting went on anyway.

Hartford told them how he'd bought the island hoping to make it into a millionaire's playground, spent $30 million, lost money, couldn't get a license, wanted a casino and a bridge. He said he was financially overextended. When the Mary Carter people left, they assured Hartford they would seriously consider it. But Mary Carter did not intend to buy the island without a guarantee that they could succeed where Hartford had failed—in obtaining a casino license. They hired themselves a lawyer—Stafford Sands.

The James Crosby version of what happened next: On their first meeting with Sands, the minister was aloof. He sat them down at a long table and expressed a distaste for Hartford, in particular for the way Hartford conducted his private life. Then he got down to business. Sands knew Mary Carter was there because it needed legal help with applications, that sort of thing. Sands didn't provide such assistance to just anyone who walked in off the street, he explained, but he told Crosby, Davis and the other Mary Carterites that he would represent them if they would agree to certain conditions. For one, he wanted them to build a specified number of hotel rooms within five years and more within ten. The executives thought that could be arranged.

Sands told them, too, that if they were granted a certificate of exemption, he would like them to have as a partner someone whom the government knew, someone who knew something about casinos. That someone would be Wallace Groves, the "logger" from the Freeport casino. They agreed to that condition as well. The minister said that obtaining the certificate should present no problem, and negotiations with Huntington Hartford were begun in earnest.

Negotiations with Hartford were prolonged and exasperating. Initially, Mary Carter thought his asking price was too high. He said he had put $30 million into the island, and they couldn't figure out where he had put it. It was nice, they thought, maybe $2 million or $3 million worth of nice. So they would ask to see the financial records to get a breakdown of what was spent where, and Hartford would say, "Ask the lawyers." Then they'd have to figure out which lawyers, there were so many, and the lawyers would all say, We don't have those books. They never did get the breakdown.

Talks dragged on for a year and a half, thanks, lawyer Charlie Murphy said, to Hartford's "childish insistence on minor points of the deal." Just when everyone thought they were in agreement, Hartford would ask for more money or he would come up with what Crosby called "quaint" little conditions of sale, and they would have to renegotiate the whole thing. The quaint little conditions were things like no hotel was allowed to be built taller than the tallest tree. Then everyone would get all worked up trying to figure out which is the tallest tree and whether to allow for growth. Then they decided it wasn't practical anyway, you couldn't make money with two-story hotels. Or he wanted them to take one statue away from his Versailles gardens or he wanted a promise that a particular beach would forever be named Hartford Beach. Everybody thought it was getting pretty tiresome, and at one point Wallace Groves said he

didn't think the deal would ever go through because of
Hartford's antics.

Once during that eighteen months, Hartford was approached by Louis Chesler, Grove's erstwhile partner in Bahamas Amusements. Chesler and Groves had had a falling out,
and Chesler offered to buy the island to turn it into a sports-
men's retreat. Hartford didn't think Chesler had enough
money and rebuffed him.

Finally, in early 1966 the Mary Carter-Groves-Hartford deal
went through. Huntington Hartford sold to the Mary Carter
Paint Company his interests in Paradise Island for $3.5 million
in cash and 250,000 shares—or 25 percent—of what would
then become a subsidiary of Mary Carter, Paradise Island Limited. In other words, Hartford would own a quarter of the parts
of Paradise Island that he was responsible for developing, including the Ocean Club, the Cafe Martinique, the golf course
and unimproved land. Hartford also bought, for $750,000 and
an agreement to loan Mary Carter $2 million, 17.6 percent of
another subsidiary, Island Hotel Company. That one owned
Paradise Island Hotel, a high rise that was under construction.
Also, Mary Carter picked up a $9 million mortgage outstand-
ing on certain portions of the property.

Hartford would later arrange a deal whereby he was entitled
to a percentage of the casino profits above $6.25 million. They
never reached that sum, and he never collected anything on it.

Hartford was confused about who was going to own the
bridge that would be built to connect Paradise Island to Nassau. It was rarely discussed. Once after a board meeting, Hartford said to Crosby, "We didn't discuss the bridge." Hartford
says that Crosby told him, "Don't worry. I'll take care of the
bridge." And he did, but not in a manner Hartford anticipated.
Crosby organized a group of private investors and some banks,
and they built the bridge with $1.8 million of their own funds.
They slapped a two-dollar toll on it (Hartford says Davis told

him it was to keep the blacks out), and the profits went to the private investors, mainly Crosby. Paradise Island and Mary Carter Paint received nothing except a dollar-a-year rental fee for the use of the land. (When I asked Crosby how the bridge has fared financially, he replied, "It has been able to survive." But most estimates put its yearly take well into the hundreds of thousands.)

Still, everyone was happy, more or less, when the island sale was completed. Wallace Groves and Mary Carter Paint signed an agreement that gave four-ninths of all the shares in the casino to Wallace Groves' Grand Bahamas Amusements and five-ninths to Mary Carter Paint. The arrangement with the government was that Mary Carter-Groves bought the certificate of exemption from the Bahamian Club in Nassau, and they would operate the casino there until their own was ready. Sir Stafford was $250,000 worth of "legal fees" richer, thanks to Mary Carter Paint. As for Hartford, he may not have been completely happy, but he didn't know it yet.

In January 1966, around the time the agreement was being consummated, Hartford received a phone call in his New York apartment, and the identity of the caller made him nervous. It was a lawyer from the organized-crime division of the U.S. Department of Justice. He wanted some information.

What did the Justice Department want with him? Hartford wondered. He didn't know anything about organized crime. He was an ordinary businessman. The caller assured him he had nothing to worry about, it was just that the department had heard he was selling some property to Mary Carter Paint Company and they wanted to talk to him about it. Would he chat?

He said he would, and he agreed to meet with investigators on Paradise Island, but it would take a few days. Hartford never traveled by plane, and the journey to the island by train and boat was a long one. About a week later, they met in Nassau.

The Justice Department was represented by two lawyers. One was David Bancroft, the other was the caller. He was Robert Peloquin.

Hartford had a ground rule. He insisted that if at any time during the day the group bumped into anyone else associated with Paradise Island, he would introduce the government boys as reporters. The lawyers thought that was silly. They had already told the Mary Carter people that they were going to interview Hartford, and the Mary Carter people obviously knew who they were. Hartford remained adamant and the lawyers agreed.

Hartford then told the lawyers his story, and when he was through, the group toured the island. Sure enough, they ran into Crosby and Davis. Hartford introduced the Justice Department lawyers as reporters. They all chatted for about five minutes, then moved on.

Robert Peloquin returned to Washington and wrote a memo to William Hundley, his boss at the Justice Department. He opined that "Huntington Hartford appears to be a bored millionaire with a childish outlook on life," but he thought Hartford would probably make a good informant. Peloquin concluded his memo with those familiar words: "Mary Carter Paints will be in control of Paradise Island with the exception of the casino which Groves will control. The atmosphere seems ripe for a Lansky skim."

Only months later, the jig was up. The Groves-Mary Carter relationship sent press and government typewriters spinning. It was great copy: little paint company buys casino, holds hands with mob. And late in the year Tex McCrary, an American public relations man operating in the Bahamas, took a tale to a couple of reporters at *The Wall Street Journal* that would eventually help topple a government and win the reporters a Pulitzer Prize.

The *Journal*, in October 1966, detailed Stafford Sands' self-dealings in the Bahamas, told about the sweetheart consultancy deals given to the members of the Executive Council that had voted to allow the Freeport casino and hinted that that casino and Grand Bahama Island might be the American mob's new sandbox. It was all the black Progressive Liberal party—the PLP—needed. They accused Stafford Sands and his "Bay Street boys" of corruption on a grand scale, demanded that a Royal Commission of Inquiry be appointed to sift through every dirty detail. They rode the scandal right into Government House.

On January 10, 1967, the PLP, in a hastily called election, won nineteen seats in government to Sir Stafford Sands' United Bahamian party's eighteen. In parliamentary fashion, the leader of the winning party acceded to the office of Premier of the Bahama Islands. The leader was Lynden O. Pindling, the first black Premier in the history of the colony.

Sir Stafford retired to Spain to pass his remaining days in disgrace—presumably comforted by wealth. Mary Carter would eventually be forced to sever its relations with Wallace Groves because in early 1967 *Life* magazine and *The Saturday Evening Post,* greatly aided in their research by Robert Peloquin at Justice, spewed forth thousands of words about the seamy circumstances surrounding the operation of Bahamian casinos.

The white government, broken, charged that it had all been a plot by the American Department of Justice. Sir Ralph Grey, the white governor of the Bahamas, summoned Robert Peloquin to his office and lambasted the lawyer for his part in the whole mess and for allowing "this bunch of baboons" to take control. Shortly after, Peloquin relates, "Poor Sir Ralph was recalled to England. Well, actually he went to Northern Ireland, and that's when that exploded."

CHAPTER TWELVE

The late sixties were a time of transition in the Bahamas, not just for the government but for Mary Carter as well. By late 1966 James Crosby was a casino executive, proud new part owner of the Bahamian Club—but it was all going awry. His partner, Wallace Groves, had been exposed in the press, and the two would have to part company. But Wallace Groves was the partner with the expertise. He was the one who knew how to run a casino. With him gone, James Crosby, paint-company executive, would be forced to take over at the Bahamian Club. What's more, there was a new, larger casino on its way on Paradise Island. He would have to tend to that one when it was ready. It was like a bachelor expecting a baby.

It was not that the Bahamian Club was not in good hands. They had seen to its welfare when they stocked the place with croupiers from the Monte Carlo Casino in Freeport and hired others from Dino Cellini's school for croupiers in London. They had installed as casino manager Eddie Cellini, a suavely handsome, strapping, tall young man who billed himself as the world's best croupier. Eddie had learned the business in illegal casinos in Kentucky and legal ones—run by Lansky—in Cuba. Resorts thought it might work out, if only the press would stop pushing the point that Eddie's brother was Dino and Dino was Meyer Lansky's right arm.

Then there was Paradise Island across the water, sitting like a pretty girl almost dressed up, no place to go. The Ocean Club was reopened, hotels were being built and the casino too. The bridge was up, a quirky-looking thing towering above the water like a great one-hump camel with curvature of the spine. These things had to be utilized. Tourists had to be brought in, roulette wheels set spinning. But how did you open a casino? How did you operate a resort?

In April of 1967, Crosby took a trip to Washington with his lawyer, Charlie Murphy, to visit the Justice Department, only two months after department-fed exposés of the islands appeared in *Life* and *The Saturday Evening Post.* The two men said they wanted advice on how to run a casino. They went to see Fred Vinson, assistant attorney general in charge of the Criminal Division, to talk about gambling. They were ushered into what Crosby called the biggest office he had ever seen, and within moments three or four other men joined them. He assumed they had been waiting. Years later he would have forgotten all but one of them—Robert Peloquin. Peloquin impressed Crosby because he seemed so knowledgeable. Actually, Crosby had met him only months before when Hartford was touring Peloquin around the island and introduced him as a reporter, but Crosby said he didn't remember that.

Crosby asked the men whom he might find to run his casino, since he had no idea how to do it himself. Peloquin was the most conversant with the problem. He said it was tough, you couldn't get a company from Nevada to operate it because they weren't allowed to run gambling operations outside that state. He asked Crosby why he didn't run it himself. Crosby says he was shocked. Nothing was resolved and he left discouraged.

But he kept thinking about Peloquin. Peloquin had handled a strike force, so he might be able to handle Crosby's casino and Crosby's fears. Three or four days after the Washington trip, Crosby and Murphy met with Peloquin again and asked him to operate the casino. It was Peloquin's turn to be shocked, but when the shock had worn off, he said he wasn't interested. Crosby urged him to travel to Paradise Island and look the place over. When Peloquin insisted he wasn't interested, Crosby told him he thought the job would justify a salary of $60,000 a year. Peloquin was interested.

Ten days later, the Justice Department official and his wife, Peggy, arrived at Paradise Island. Peloquin later came to call it "the crying weekend" because that was how his wife spent most of it. She did not like the idea of raising her six children on a tropical island. Peloquin was torn. Sixty thousand dollars was two and a half times his government salary. He thought it was a spectacular offer, a once-in-a-lifetime opportunity. He awoke one night at midnight and walked the beach until dawn, pondering his future. When he got back to his room, his wife was in a panic—she thought he had been kidnapped. That seemed to settle it. Peloquin told Crosby, Thank you, no.

Mary Carter eventually wound up announcing that it would run the controversial casino itself, but it wasn't long before they had some help because within months Robert Peloquin showed up with his new law partner, William Hundley. They proposed adding Mary Carter to their list of clients, which already included the National Football League and *Life* magazine. In October 1967, Mary Carter retained the law firm of Hundley and Peloquin.

One of the lawyers' early duties was to set up a security system. The other was to make sure that no casino employees were members of organized crime or mob-influenced. They were not wholly successful at either endeavor.

In the magic month of December 1967, the Paradise Island Casino opened with a hoopla-filled party chockful of society types, a handful of not-quite movie stars, like Janet Leigh (a frequent companion of Jack Davis), lights, music, dancing, loud fun and a guest of honor, a has-been, some said, not worth bothering with. He was Richard Nixon. It was a dizzying occasion, an auspicious start. Paradise Island was launched.

The following April there was another bash, a whole weekend to celebrate—none of the guests were quite certain what. It might have something to do with a new hotel, they thought, but it didn't matter, they all knew how they had gotten there. No such weekend would have been complete without a smattering of beautiful people and a celebrity or two, so a publicity person had been hired, the royal white Russian Serge Obolenski. He was *the* society public relations man and perfectly capable of stocking almost any party with the most beautiful people of the time on a moment's notice—especially if it was somewhere tropical and it was free! And so they came, twittering in from all over the world to fill the island, a Vanderbilt or two, gossip columnist Suzy, Princess Pignatelli, the maharajah of Jaipur, the marquis de Merry del Val, Mrs. Nan Kempner of best-dressed fame, Lord Lichfield, Carol Channing, Art Linkletter, and yes, Richard Nixon dropped by too.

The weekend was chronicled in fascinating detail in many a gossip column. *Look* magazine headlined its coverage DARLING HOW DIVINE! ANOTHER JUNKET WITH THE BEAUTIFUL PEOPLE! and described some of the weekend's delights, like, "The next morning there is some confusion at the coffee shop because there doesn't seem to be any coffee—only bagels. Gracious, what would a beautiful person want with a bagel?"

CHAPTER THIRTEEN

After all the beautiful people faded away, it was left to Mary Carter Paint to go about the business of running a casino. By mid-1968, the company was ten years into its newest Crosby family-controlled incarnation. Here is what it owned: the Paradise Island Hotel and villas, one reconditioned, re-opened championship golf course, one recently expanded casino, the Beach Inn, the Cafe Martinique, sundry other restaurants, a partially built Britannia Beach Hotel, the Ocean Club and land on Paradise Island and Grand Bahama Island.

Here's what Mary Carter didn't own: Mary Carter. It was dumped in May. That dream acquisition, that little concern in which Crosby had placed such faith only a decade earlier, was sold, from the lowliest can of paint to the biggest factory. That bountiful business had not been one of the great success stories of modern American business—it was losing market share. When it was sold, with it went its name—you couldn't use a paint-company name without a paint company.

In the early summer of 1968, Resorts International was born. Chairman James Crosby envisioned a dazzling, conti-nent-spanning, globe-encircling resort-casino complex. The name Resorts International would be associated with all of the great glamour capitals of the world. As it turned out, they never quite made it to the glamour capitals, but they visited some exotic places in their quest. One was Tunisia. They were invited by the President to discuss a resort development, but they never made a proposal. Then there was a potential deal for a casino outside Athens, and another one in Yugoslavia. They weren't interested. Someone introduced them to the rulers of the Philippines, the Marcos family, and there was talk about a casino and resort outside Manila. It didn't work out. Another possibility was Haiti. They had in mind a semi-industrial resort-residential complex, a kind of base for the supertankers that come up from Venezuela. They made a proposal to the government, but the government never got back to them. (Years later, a Washington *Post* story charged that Resorts had tried to bribe Papa Doc Duvalier for the right to open a casino in Haiti. Resorts denied it.) Sy Alter introduced them to another possibility in Honduras. They were going to lease a million-acre tract of totally undeveloped, very wild land and tame it into a vast development that re-created Africa. They inspected it, ventured a few ideas, started negotiating with the government. Before negotiations were through, Honduras went to war, and that was the end of that.

For a long time, Paradise Island would remain at the heart of the company's business. There were sidelines, to be sure—Biff-Burger, for one. That was an acquisition that turned out to be one of the few turkeys in the early fast-food–beef business. It operated differently from the others in that its outlets were movable. If a specific roadside site didn't prove successful, they simply picked it up and moved it elsewhere. It never worked and eventually they chucked it. They turned down an opportunity to get involved in Kentucky Fried Chicken when that business was just being hatched.

Then there was the shrimp-farming business, the cultivation of shrimp in artificial surroundings. They insisted that would have been very profitable and they would have made money if only they had stayed at it longer. But they sold it to Coca-Cola. They also bought and eventually sold Tennis United, an instructional tennis facility located under the Fifty-ninth Street Bridge in Manhattan.

One of Resorts' more controversial acquisitions was the 1974 purchase of Chalk's International Airline, which billed itself as the oldest airline in the world. It ran seaplanes from Paradise Island to just outside Miami proper, and had a route okay to Cuba. Chalk's was bought from Edward Dixon, a friend of James Crosby's, who sold it to the company when he was in trouble with the IRS. Dixon pleaded no contest to the charges —his lawyer, by the way, was Robert Peloquin—and served seven months in jail. He didn't repay the money he owed the government. Dixon had links to corrupt Pennsylvania Representative Daniel Flood, and his family's name had been connected with improprieties involving contracts to put out coal-mine fires in Pennsylvania. Resorts bought the Chalk's airline for $30,000, though estimates valued its supply of planes in the hundreds of thousands, possibly millions. It seemed odd that when Crosby's friend was in trouble, Crosby bought his airline at a fraction of its true value. The cheap price led New Jersey investigators, among many others, to speculate that in fact Resorts had paid much more, but that for appearances' sake they claimed less. That way, the IRS would not try to attach Dixon's funds to satisfy the amount he owed them.

The casino, for its part, managed to escape many of the financial, if not the bad-press, problems of its brother subsidiaries. Most years it managed to make more money than the others managed to lose. Still, running a casino was a difficult task made more so because despite its original associations, Resorts suddenly found itself on an island in the middle of a foreign country that was not as friendly as it had been a year or two before. The reason was a new government that was experiencing growing pains and was not convinced that Resorts International was on its side. Resorts had painstakingly greased the right legal palms and had chosen the right business bedfellows when it first arrived on the island, but they were only the right ones in the eyes of Stafford Sands and he didn't count anymore. After carefully laying the groundwork, the company found that half of its teammates were suddenly gone and the opposing team had added some mighty big new players, angry ones at that.

Resorts International was not the only nervous company. The Prime Minister of the Bahamas, Lynden Pindling, delivered his famous "bend or break" speech, in which he declared that if foreign companies didn't bend, if they didn't make large concessions to the people of the Bahamas—they would be broken. Bahamians were not going to be just waiters and waitresses in hotels, they were going to be bankers, they were going to have positions of responsibility.

A comic strip of the aftermath of that speech might have shown grown imperialists overturning drawers into suitcases and grabbing toothbrushes and selling or closing down businesses so they could get out on the next boat. Many businessmen were convinced that black governments could not be dealt with.

Resorts International took another tack. They learned very quickly that black governments could be paid off just as easily as white ones. The Resorts executives would never be particularly liked or trusted by the government, especially not Davis and his righthand man, Steve Norton—Pindling thought they were racists. But they might learn to fairly peacefully coexist.

If the government was displeased, there were any number of things they could do to make life miserable. Customs, for one, could be a problem. Imagine trying to equip several hotels, a handful of restaurants and a casino almost entirely dependent on imports for food and furniture and slot machines, and having problems with customs. On that one, Sy Alter was very helpful.

Alter was the only non-Bahamian member of a small social club, the Coyaba Club, which counted bridge among its activities. A lot of the members of the club were customs officials. One day Sy Alter and Resorts president Jack Davis decided that something nice ought to be done for these men who were responsible for allowing through, in a three-year period, 150 million pounds of what Davis called "everything from peas and carrots to steel girders." So Alter took some of the guys on a little trip to Las Vegas, where he wined them, dined them and supplied them with $650 worth of what he captioned on his expense voucher as "girls."

Jack Davis says he asked Alter what "girls" was for. Alter explained that the men had run out of money and had approached him for some funds for entertainment of female companions (or, bluntly put, hookers). He felt he was in a position where he had to contribute, so he bankrolled their extracurricular activities. Years later, Davis would claim that Resorts had refused to reimburse Sy for the call-girl expenses; it was not proper allocation of corporate funds, and Alter would have to take it out of his own pocket. Alter said he understood, says Davis.

If that was the position Resorts took, the company was drawing some very fine lines in both a moral and a financial sense. The trip was so successful that it was followed by others to Las Vegas and Acapulco. And later on, too, a slush fund—unrecorded on the books—was set up, dedicating thousands of dollars of cash and other gifts to government officials. Some money went to what James Crosby called "low-level orgies." The money, in addition to not being properly recorded on the books of the company, was not reported to the SEC for many years, and Resorts didn't bother discussing it with the company financial vice-president, Raymond Gore, until 1976.

If lower-level officials got watches and girls, it was in the best tradition of the competitive capitalistic-political incentive system that the higher you rose, the more you got. Prime Minister Pindling got a $40,000 Rolls-Royce, thanks in part to a several-thousand-dollar gift from Resorts. (Resorts was by no means the Prime Minister's only benefactor. Days after he was elected, Pindling moved from a modest home into a million-dollar mansion. The rumor that won't be quashed is that he had Robert Vesco to thank for that one.)

Resorts also made hundreds of thousands of dollars of "political contributions" to Pindling's party and, to hedge its bets, to his opposition. These were sometimes made in cash and sometimes delivered personally by Jack Davis. Often, the funds were laundered through a local law firm and Sy Alter's paychecks. At times the company carried them on its books as "legal expenses." Crosby said the payments were made so that Resorts could help "preserve the two-party system."

As for "girls," Sy Alter has often been heard to brag about the ones he supplies to Crosby. Jack Davis exhibited an eye for detail when it came to insuring that the prostitutes hanging around Paradise Island were diverting enough. On at least one occasion, Davis decided that the ladies who worked the casino had seen one night too many, and he phoned to Miami for fresh recruits. The older ones would be purged from the casino. One of those hapless hookers, a working woman named Lulu, managed to make herself an exception to the casino rule.

Lulu's base of operations was a stool in the Birdcage Lounge overlooking the Paradise Island Casino. She was a Bahamian native, an independent businesswoman who was pretty satisfied with her work and wasn't ready to give it up when the casino tried to hand her her street-walking papers. But Lulu's brother was a fire-department inspector, and shortly after his sister was bounced, he showed up at the casino and conducted a "routine" fire inspection, finding many violations. It was nothing you could take care of overnight; they were the kinds of things that might even mean closing the casino.

The story, of course, has a happy ending. Lulu stayed at her perch in the Birdcage Lounge, the fire violations mysteriously disappeared and the casino remained open.

If Lulu won out over Resorts International, Sy Alter poked similar fun at some of the higher-ups in the Bahamian government. Alter was of the belief that Bahamian men prided themselves on their superior masculinity. He was not above a practical joke in capitalizing on that belief. Alter let drop to some government officials that he had discovered a magical potion that made a man, well, manlier. The way it worked was, it made him swell. The officials were at first skeptical. What would Sy discover next, the Fountain of Youth? Alter told them that to show them he was dealing in good faith, he would let them try some of the stuff, no strings attached. He doled out the sugar water, or whatever it was, then found a couple of hookers and arranged to have them in the right place at the right time and really ham it up, with Academy Award-winning squealing and groaning. It worked. The men were soon back for more.

CHAPTER FOURTEEN

One more precaution Resorts International took against disharmony with the Bahamian government was David Probinsky, a public relations man. Probinsky was a high school dropout from the New Jersey shore town of Wildwood who began his career working in bars and liquor stores in that area and eventually came to credit himself with pioneering civil rights in the United States, all but singlehandedly electing a government in the Bahamas—and changing the fortunes of Resorts International. Eventually, too, he would play a real-life Monopoly game in which not only would he get a million dollars without passing Go, but he would get it for doing a public relations job that involved *not* talking.

His story goes like this: After leaving school, he continued to live mostly in the Wildwood area, dabbling in real estate and picking up an interest in a black club (Probinsky is white), the Esquire Club, that operated only in the summer months.

In the late fifties in Florida, Probinsky met Sam Rabin, the owner of the Sir John, a large Miami hotel that catered to a black clientele. Rabin hired Probinsky because of his "expertise in dealing with black people." The Sir John was one of the leading black hotels in the country. People like Sammy Davis,

Jr., Joe Louis and Martin Luther King, who could not get into other hotels in Miami, stayed there. During the time Probinsky was at the Sir John, celebrated black people were constantly in and out, including prominent political and business men from the Caribbean area as well as from Latin America. At times, the State Department also put prominent Africans up at the Sir John.

With the sixties came strides in civil rights, and as segregation began to crack, so, too, did the necessity for the Sir John. The people who had once stayed there now went to Miami Beach. The Sir John went bankrupt.

Probinsky spent six months depressed about his life and his dismal financial state. He had not lost everything with the demise of the hotel, though. Surviving intact were friendships with people like Gerald Cash, who would later be knighted and become governor of the Bahamas; powerful Florida lawyers, like Henry Arrington; and one soon to be a very important politician in the Bahamas, Lynden O. Pindling.

Probinsky found a new job doing public relations for Champale, the company that made the drink touted as tasting like champagne at ginger ale prices. Champale needed distribution in the Bahamas, and they thought Probinsky's connections might prove useful. He took the job, but with a double motive, he says. He had heard that there might be an election in 1967, and he figured it was his chance to travel, at Champale's expense, to the outlying islands of the Bahamas and "get a feel for what the hell was going on." He had never been politically active in the islands.

Probinsky severed his relationship with Champale soon after lawyer Henry Arrington arranged for him to deliver a package to Lynden Pindling—then member of Parliament in the Bahamas and leader of the Progressive Liberal party—so Probinsky could get acquainted with him. Perhaps Probinsky could help in Pindling's campaign. Probinsky had a couple of points in his favor. He had been active, in earlier years, in New Jersey politics and had been chairman of the Young Democrats in the Republican stronghold areas of Wildwood and Cape May County. He was also campaign manager for George James, who later became his lawyer, as well as for all the other Democrats who ran. (He had also, by that time, met Marvin Perskie, a New Jersey lawyer who would be a rung on Probinsky's million-dollar ladder.)

Probinsky's other asset was a working knowledge of the Bahamas. He had visited the islands often during his Sir John days. He did business with Freddy Munnings, the operator of an elaborate black nightclub in Nassau, The Cat and the Fiddle. Probinsky had run a big black review at the Sir John, and he and Munnings often traded performers, which required that Probinsky travel back and forth to look at the acts and book shows.

But his knowledge of the Bahamas was of no great importance when Probinsky was appointed Pindling's campaign manager, because the PLP made clear that his chief duty would be to raise funds outside the Bahamas. After all, he was white, and it wouldn't look right for a white man to be campaign manager for a black party.

One of the first people he approached, he says, was Michael McLaney, a Florida businessman who had been in and out of the gambling business for a large part of his adult life, in Cuba mostly, and for a while at the Cat Cay Club in the Bahamas. McLaney was alleged to have ties to Meyer Lansky, which makes some interested observers skeptical about Probinsky's story of how he came to meet the man.

Probinsky says he was in Miami getting some campaign materials prepared by a printer of Cuban extraction. In the course of chatting with the printer about the job, Probinsky said, By the way, did the printer know anyone who had a spare few hundred thousand lying around that he would like to kick in to the campaign of a man who probably wouldn't win? The Cuban said sure, he knew a guy who might be interested. "In fact, he owns a small interest in this print shop."

The printer phoned McLaney at home. His wife said he wasn't there, he was at the airport, so they had him paged. According to Probinsky, McLaney said he would "delay his flight to wherever he was going and we would get the hell over there and talk to him."

According to Probinsky, McLaney was not amicably inclined toward Stafford Sands and the Bay Street boys. He felt they had hammered him royally, that they had forced him out of the Cat Cay casino. He said he would do almost anything to get revenge, but supporting Pindling seemed a bit much because, as McLaney told Probinsky, "you know, everybody in Miami, everybody in the world doesn't believe that Pindling and the PLP have a chance."

He asked Probinsky for statistics—constituencies, breakdowns on who was running and where—to show to some friends who might be able to help. Probinsky got the information together, gave it to McLaney, and a week or two later McLaney called and said, "I've got a few hundred dollars for you, just to get things started." The two men met several more times, but Probinsky didn't think McLaney was interested: "He was interested in some club he belonged to and he fancied himself quite a sportsman and he played golf and tennis and hobnobbed with all these famous personalities."

Later, says Probinsky, he learned that McLaney made his living gambling and playing golf, and that he was having a problem hanging on to his home, an enormous place. But McLaney eventually managed to come up with around ten or fifteen thousand dollars. He gave it to Probinsky in checks, always reminding him not to cash it until he called or to "take it to this bank or deposit it in that bank in a system," said Probinsky, "that is commonly known as 'kiting checks.'"

The contributions were enough to warrant a phone call by Probinsky to Pindling, who was in London "discussing Parliamentary procedure." Probinsky told the politician about the money, and Pindling said, "I think you're rushing this thing too much. I don't see how we are going to have an election before April or May." He added that this fellow McLaney, whom he had heard about, frightened him.

Probinsky went to Pindling later and told him that before McLaney would come up with any decent money, he wanted to meet with Pindling. They arranged to meet at an airport hotel in Miami, but on the way there, Pindling said he was "scared to death." He couldn't explain why, he was just uncomfortable about McLaney. He wanted to call it off until they could further check him out.

Probinsky said, "Gosh, he told me you were his attorney."

Pindling said, "I am, but I only met him once. It's nothing to do with political things."

The meeting was called off, said Probinsky, and he asked Henry Arrington to investigate McLaney. Arrington called around to some friends in law enforcement and came back with, "Every report I have on McLaney is okay. He's always been on the fringe of things, but I don't—there's nothing, I think, that Pindling should be disturbed about."

When Pindling, Probinsky and McLaney finally met at McLaney's mansion, McLaney talked nonstop, said Probinsky, "about everything from this and that in the inception," including how the reigning party in the Bahamas had wronged him. Finally Pindling said, "Well, Mike, I know you're not in this for laughs, so what do you want out of it?" Mike said he would like a little casino or two or three. Pindling explained that the PLP opposed casinos, since a lot of their members were Baptists. He added, though, that he could see how the government could make a lot of money out of it, but still, he thought the government should own the casinos.

He must have said something more reassuring, because McLaney later dug up lots more money. Shortly after Pindling's victory in early 1967, Probinsky moved into an office next door to the Premier's at Lawson Square and began to act as Pindling's press agent, dealing with the hordes of reporters that he said were "swarming down to the Bahamas." Later the government hired a big New York public relations firm to handle that sort of thing, and Probinsky, with some government officials, set up his own PR firm. But he remained on friendly terms with the new Premier.

Mike McLaney was not so lucky. A boat was discovered offshore of the Bahamas, filled to the brim with gambling equipment, and despite his denials, everyone thought it belonged to McLaney. Then, early in his reign, Pindling sought advice from the Justice Department on who might not be "desirables" in the Bahamas. He was particularly worried about four people—public relations man Tex McCrary (who spilled the beans to *The Wall Street Journal*), David Probinsky, Mike McLaney and Louis Chesler. The Justice Department sent Robert Peloquin to advise the Premier. Peloquin detailed the men's backgrounds, and when he was finished, said Peloquin, Pindling told him he would be sure that "Chesler, McLaney and Probinsky gained no positions of influence through his government."

A few days later, Tex McCrary told Peloquin that Pindling had ordered McLaney and Probinsky to leave the islands. It was only half-true. McLaney left, threatening to sue *Life* magazine for its part in his downfall. Probinsky may have left until the situation cooled, but he was soon back, as close as ever to Pindling. That friendship, and his business partnership with other members of government, was one good reason why by 1968 Probinsky had a new client: Resorts International.

CHAPTER FIFTEEN

Some companies have trouble getting publicity. Resorts had trouble avoiding it, especially when it was least welcome. In all of its guises—Resorts International, Mary Carter Paint, Paradise Island—the company was an unending source of fascination to reporters. In 1969, for example, the press began jumping all over it because that was the year, with Resorts barely settled into Paradise Island, eking out $3 million in earnings and trading on the also-ran American Stock Exchange, that the company launched into its guppy-swallowing-the-whale routine. It tried to buy Pan Am, one of the world's largest airlines, with $60 million in earnings and over $1 billion in sales.

The way it started, according to Crosby, is that he and his friend Charles Bludhorn, chairman of colossal conglomerate Gulf and Western, were passing the time together in the sun one day on Paradise Island. Bludhorn mentioned that his company was sitting on close to 2 million shares of Pan Am stock —around 5 percent of the total. Crosby said he'd like to have some of it. Resorts had an abiding interest in airlines. (Over the years they have bought a number of them, little ones mostly, like Palm Tree Airlines, Amphibious Airways and Chalk's.)

Pan Am was in businesses that Crosby thought were compatible with his own. They had hotels and resorts with casinos, and most of all, they had airplanes to take people to all those places. Hypothetically, they could take junket players to gambling resorts.

Crosby offered to buy some of the stock. He wanted to buy half the shares outright and take an option on the other half. His offer was accepted, and Resorts International agreed to pay Gulf and Western $16 million in cash and 500,000 shares of Resorts International Class A stock in return for 900,000 shares of Pan Am. The transaction was valued at $39 million.

Soon after, Crosby got a tip from his buddies at the go-go Beverly Hills brokerage firm of Kleiner Bell and Company (which would later be put out of business by the SEC) that Chase Manhattan, fifth largest bank in the United States, owned a huge block of Pan Am stock too, in its trust department. Resorts tried to interest the bank in selling its shares in a noncash deal—by trading stock, for example. At the time, cash was not something Resorts International had plenty of.

It was not the kind of decision a thoughtful bank dealing with a conservatively run trust department could make offhandedly. Chase sent three of its crackerjack research analysts down to Paradise Island to talk to management, evaluate the proposal, get a feel for the situation. The analysts' financial reason may have been bent somewhat by the tropical air, their business senses dulled by the lapping waves. They had a good time—Resorts saw to that. Recalls a fellow worker: "Those guys came back just raving about the place. They made quite a few more trips. They were very well treated—wined and dined and supplied with who knows what else. There was lots of guffawing in the halls at the bank, and lots of rumors circulating. They became very tight with Resorts' management. The upshot was they recommended the bank do a deal."

It was a complicated financing package. Chase agreed to sell

Resorts 1.5 million shares of Pan Am stock for what amounted, in effect, to IOUs and options: Chase would accept $15 million worth of subordinated 5 percent, 25-year notes and 15-year warrants to purchase 3 million Resorts Class A shares, half at $40 a share and the rest at $60 a share. In mid-February 1969, when the negotiations were going on, those Resorts shares were selling at $56. Two weeks later they had plunged to $45. Pan Am slipped from $27 to $25.

No sooner had the deal been consummated than it created a furor that spread from the Bahamas to Beverly Hills, from Wall Street to Washington. Pan Am decried this little upstart, this insignificant corporate presence having the gall to try to take over no less a corporate giant than Pan Am. The debate carried clear to the halls of Congress, where legislators stood in the aisles and launched tirades. Soley on the strength of that one attempted transaction, a bill was introduced in Congress that forbade non-airlines from owning more than 5 percent of any airline's stock.

The American Stock Exchange was forced to act. In March it halted trading in Resorts International stock pending a more orderly market. Everyone was trying to sell. The price of the stock had plummeted to $34. The halt lasted three weeks.

Then the SEC jumped into the fray, demanding to know what, exactly, Resorts had in mind and why Chase had handed over the Pan Am stock on terms that amounted to a loan. Resorts was cowed, a little. It staunchly defended its actions, took umbrage with those that would accuse it of ulterior motives. It did, however, cut back the number of shares by nearly half.

The deal went through in mid-April. Resorts' shares had recovered somewhat, to $43, but a long, unbroken downward slide was not long in coming. When the storm clouds ultimately rolled by, nearly everyone involved in the deal had taken a soaking. As mentioned, Resorts wound up feuding with the

SEC over the value of its Pan Am holdings. The stock price was not what it had been when the acquisition occurred, and in 1974 the SEC finally forced the company to write down the value of the holdings on its books. That write-down was most of the reason why Resorts lost $6 a share in 1974.

Chase had accepted warrants, a form of option, to buy the stock at $40 and $60, levels it would not reach until long after Chase had sold them. And there were less tangible costs. The face of David Rockefeller, Chase Manhattan's chairman, must have been awfully red, because one of his large corporate clients was Pan Am. Chase had made a fool of itself in the eyes of the client and the financial community. No mathematician could have found a way to put a figure on the damage the bank had done to its own reputation. As for Resorts, in some ways it was just one more episode in a corporate history full of episodes. It would be eclipsed only months later by the firing of Eddie Cellini.

CHAPTER SIXTEEN

Eddie Cellini was a damned good casino manager. No one contested that. Almost nobody disagreed with him when he called himself the world's best croupier. Resorts' faith in him had been such that he was given sole responsibility for the hiring of casino employees. None of that was what bothered the ever-present press. Reporters were more interested in that same old story: Eddie Cellini was the brother of Meyer Lansky aide Dino Cellini, and Dino Cellini was bad news.

Resorts said Eddie was nothing like Dino. Eddie was honest and hard-working, and for all they knew, Dino and Eddie never associated with each other. Some people had a hard time swallowing that. Eddie, like Dino, practically grew up in casinos. He worked at the Hotel Nacional in Havana from 1957 until Castro closed it down two years later. Then, as noted, and by his own admission, he was involved in illegal casinos in Ohio and Kentucky, two hotbeds of mid-century illegal gambling in the United States.

In 1964 Eddie Cellini took a job at the Monte Carlo Casino in Freeport, the alleged Lansky place where Dino was also employed. In 1967 Eddie was one of the employees transferred from the Monte Carlo to the Bahamian Club in Nassau—the joint venture of Resorts International and Wallace Groves—and a short while later he went to the Paradise Island Casino. His brother had been expelled from the islands by the government. In 1967 Dino was routed from England, where he had been running a school for croupiers. Resorts asked the British government to allow Eddie to continue in Dino's place, but it refused. In 1968, in fact, Eddie was banned from entering Britain, a process known as "stop-listing." That same year, according to the president of Bally, the manufacturer of gambling equipment, Dino received a commission of $28,200 for selling slot machines to Paradise Island.

In testimony in the *Rolling Stone*-Resorts International libel suit, Vincent Teresa, an organized-crime figure whose testimony led to the conviction of a multitude of other crime figures, said that he once tapped Dino Cellini and Meyer Lansky for help in setting himself up as a junket manager to Paradise Island. (A junket manager arranges for big gamblers to take all-expenses-paid trips to casinos on the premise that they'll lose enough at the tables to make it worth the casino's while.) Teresa said that Lansky instructed Dino to talk to his brother Eddie and make arrangements for complimentary accommodations on Paradise Island. According to Teresa, Dino did so.

In December 1967, Resorts International signed a three-year contract with Eddie Cellini. As manager of the Paradise Island Casino, he was promised a salary and a percentage of casino profits over a certain amount. In November 1969, the government of the Bahamas stop-listed Eddie and he was ordered to leave the islands. Resorts says it fired Eddie before he was forced to leave. The problem was that the press still hovered over Paradise Island like so many circling buzzards. Every time the name Paradise Island was mentioned in print, the accompanying text would note that it was the place that had the casino that had the manager whose sibling was "notorious."

It was so embarrassing that one day in 1969, Crosby, relates the company, told Peloquin to get rid of Eddie. What he actually said, according to Peloquin, and depending on to whom Peloquin is telling the story, was, "I don't care if he's the Pope, dump him," or "I don't care if he's St. Peter, can him." So he was canned—except he wasn't. He continued to work for the company in Miami, often frequented their Arthur Godfrey Road offices, and on at least one occasion did a special project for them that involved surveying another casino. The terms of his contract were fulfilled. For the three-year period ending December 1970, Cellini was paid $450,000.

But he *was* banished from Paradise, and not everyone thought it was fair. Said Peloquin: "I found Edward Cellini to be an outstanding individual. I think if Edward Cellini was born in a different atmosphere, he could well be sitting as a judge in New Jersey or on the board of General Motors or possibly the archbishop of Philadelphia." Besides, says Peloquin, "why does everybody always talk about his brother Dino? Why don't they talk about his sister, the mother superior?"

Huntington Hartford was sad too. "I kind of liked Eddie," he said. "He was good-looking, businesslike, tall." Be that as it may, Eddie Cellini was soon replaced in reporters' affections by someone who provided even more interesting copy.

CHAPTER SEVENTEEN

The spate of FBI telegrams that ricocheted back and forth in November of 1970 on a triangular axis from Las Vegas to Miami to Washington were stamped URGENT. The subject was a missing person, one of the most notorious of modern times: Howard Hughes. On Thanksgiving night, November 26, Hughes had vanished from Las Vegas, swiftly and mysteriously. His top aide, Robert Maheu, claimed his boss had been kidnapped by members of his own organization who were jockeying for control of the Croesus-like Hughes empire.

Even the FBI was stymied. They relied heavily on the press for information, including one report that had it that Hughes had materialized in Nassau, which turned out to be true. Robert Maheu had been ejected from his position as chief of Hughes' Nevada operations, and Hughes had been spirited away to the islands.

The details of the removal of Hughes would always remain hazy. A Lockheed jet had somehow gotten the go-ahead to land at an Air Force base near Las Vegas, and Hughes had been hustled out of his Desert Inn in Vegas and flown to Nassau. Destination: the Britannia Beach Hotel, Paradise Island, a hotel belonging to Resorts International.

Maybe it was coincidence, that choice of hotel, and maybe not. Those same FBI memos detailed an event that had occurred shortly before the Hughes reencampment and before Maheu was fired:

> In connection with removal of Maheu . . . it has been announced by Davis and Gay [Hughes executives] that "Intertel" will be engaged on contract basis by Hughes organization to operate security and certain management phases of Nevada casino-hotels owned by Hughes. "Intertel" is code name for International Intelligence Services, Inc., described as "distinguished international company of experts on intelligence and security" headed by Robert D. Peloquin, president and chief of Department of Justice's first organized crime strike force. As Bureau is aware, Peloquin is former Department assistant of William G. Hundley, former head of Department's Organized Crime and Racketeering section. Peloquin and Hundley are partners in law firm and Hundley is officer of Intertel. Intertel reportedly originally financed to extent of about two million by Resorts International, Inc., which has substantial gambling interests in Bahamas.

Nevada Governor Paul Laxalt fretted to the press that the attempted takeover of the Hughes empire by some of his executives was of great concern to the state. Everybody wanted to know who Intertel was and where it came from. The FBI speculated that Intertel might become a substantial operating presence in Nevada gambling, and requested all available information on both Intertel and Resorts International from agency branches. One FBI memo noted that a Hughes Nevada official had stated that "Mary Carter Paint Company and Resorts International may possibly be hoodlum infiltrated or financially indebted to Meyer Lansky."

Meanwhile, down on Paradise Island, the waves continued to lick the shore and the sun went on shining and life was probably a lot calmer than it was in Nevada. Tourists had a new pastime—staring up at the ninth-floor windows of the Britannia Beach Hotel and wondering if all of the intriguing speculation was true. The entire floor had been rented to a single party, and weeks in advance, a special telephone system was installed so that calls could be made to the States without switchboard interference.

Resorts president Jack Davis was in residence in his office on the ground floor, and he made colorful, quotable quotes to the flocking reporters to the effect that he didn't know who was up there, but whoever he was, he paid his bills. It made good copy, but it seemed highly unlikely Davis didn't know the identity of the mysterious visitor, because the visitor had a new protector, Intertel. Jack Davis was the president of Resorts International, and Resorts International was the parent of Intertel.

Robert Peloquin had come a long way since that dawn on Paradise Island when he walked the beach and pondered his future. Like many bright young lawyers, he had gone through the revolving door between government service and private practice. Bright young lawyers graduate from school, find employment at some federal agency, put in three or four years at scratch wages, then more than make up for it when they are warmly welcomed by prominent Washington or Wall Street law firms or corporations that are regulated. The bright young lawyers are valuable because they know, inside out, the agencies their clients must deal with.

There are abuses in the system. There are persuasions, some subtle, some less so, for young lawyers to behave in certain ways toward certain companies while inside. They may not succumb, but some do because they have their future to consider.

Robert Peloquin was a part of that system, but he took it further. He turned it into an art form when he started Intertel, the security force which was billed as "a unique consulting organization to safeguard business from the hidden risks of vulnerability to criminal elements." Its scare-tactic logo: "The Legitimate Business: Prime Target of Organized Crime."

All Intertel contracts would be oral. The organization would concern itself with everything from controlling security at the Mullet Bay Casino of its first client, Henry Ford, to what Peloquin called "trying to find the son of a corporate executive who wandered into Khyber Pass and never came out," to overseeing airport security systems.

Peloquin stocked Intertel with former representatives of every important federal agency and a number of tactical state and city law enforcement offices as well. Officers included Thomas J. McKeon, former chief, U.S. Department of Justice Organized Crime Strike Force, Detroit; William A. Kolar, former director of the Internal Security and Intelligence divisions of the IRS; John D. O'Connell, former special agent and intelligence supervisor, FBI.

Also on the payroll was Fenelon A. Richards, who had been the director of enforcement of the U.S. Bureau of Customs. He spoke fluent Spanish, which would be useful in handling the post-mortem affairs of Howard Hughes. Gary L. Gardner was former counsel to the New Jersey State Commission of Investigation. James O. Golden had been a special agent in the U.S. Secret Service, a favorite Nixon Secret Service man and director of security at the 1968 Republican convention.

On the Intertel board of directors, among others, was Sir Ranulph Bacon, former president of the Royal Commission of Inquiry into gambling in the Bahamas. His report had cast a skeptical eye on Mary Carter Paint.

Intertel is quick to point out that it never hired anyone out of public service until they first "retired." But these people were not sixty-five years old; most were in the prime of their careers. They were taking with them great stores of knowledge on how their agencies worked, and they were leaving behind invaluable contacts. Intertel, and thus Resorts International, gave itself a line in on every law enforcement body that might make a difference. As a man who had once butted up against them put it, "They hired the strike force."

There were some law enforcement people, however, who thought that despite it all, Intertel was inept and had a way of bungling its duties. They thought it exhibited a willingness to let Resorts deal with those so-called enemies of legitimate business when it was expedient.

There were others who considered Intertel a sinister, mysterious spy-for-hire shop, an evil body capable of anything. An IRS agent once held a top-secret meeting at the Britannia Beach Hotel on Paradise Island. Within two days of the session, he learned that an account of the meeting had leaked out that was so precise as to leave little doubt it had been taped. The agent suspected Intertel.

Intertel and Peloquin and their close relationships to government agencies were of concern to some within those agencies. One worried government memo dealt with Peloquin's ties to the Justice Department. In 1968, while Peloquin was retained by the NFL as a lawyer, he wrote a memo to the league commissioner, Pete Rozelle, detailing a pending federal grand jury investigation in Alexandria, Virginia, into gambling allegations involving pro football players. The investigation was being conducted by Peloquin's former employer, the Justice Department. Peloquin's memo revealed an intimate knowledge of the investigation, even though it was supposed to be confidential.

At one point in the investigation, grand jury subpoenas were issued for several of the ballplayers but were withdrawn before they were served. An IRS agent assigned to the investigation charged that there was interference in his attempts to get at the truth.

The strangest case was that of Sante Bario and Operation

Croupier. In 1974, Philip Smith, a regional director of the U.S. Drug Enforcement Agency, recommended to his acting chief that a covert intelligence project be mounted in the Caribbean because he had received "reliable" information that croupiers at gambling casinos in the area were engaged in drug smuggling. A special agent of the DEA, Sante Bario, reported later that Smith told him the source of the information was Intertel, and that croupiers in the Paradise Island Casino were among those smuggling drugs. The inference is that Intertel could not handle problems with its own casino. It should be noted that years earlier, Smith worked with Peloquin on a government strike force and had once accepted a job with Intertel, which he later declined.

When the investigation, Operation Croupier, was launched, Sante Bario was assigned undercover in Paradise Island. (Intertel, incidentally, had employed Bario in 1971 on a security project in a Las Vegas casino.)

Bario spent two weeks in Nassau conducting the operation. He gambled and lost $605, which he included on an expense voucher upon his return. An assistant to DEA official Lucien Conein asked Bario to delete the gambling expenses from his voucher and then repaid him in cash. Bario asked where the money came from but got no reply. The assistant further requested that Bario rewrite his report of the investigation. Bario refused; he had already submitted it to Conein's office to be retyped in final form. But Bario never saw the report in final form. Other DEA officials later found that deleted from the report were all references to Bario's gambling, plus references to "possible integrity violations"—such as cheating, perhaps—by Paradise Island Casino croupiers.

The story got more bizarre years later. Bario, who had a good record as an investigator in several areas of law enforcement—IRS, New York City's Knapp Commission and DEA—wound up in jail. A long-time DEA informant had helped Bario set up a raid in Mexico City that netted thirty-three pounds of Colombian cocaine. Bario turned in twenty-two pounds to the DEA and let the informant keep the rest. Bario insisted later that it was standard operating procedure—allowing an informant to keep part of the haul was the price paid for his loyalty. The informant stated that Bario had given it to him to sell and that they would split the take. Bario was arrested and held on $500,000 bail.

On a December evening in 1978, Sante Bario, in his jail cell, was served a peanut-butter sandwich. He took one bite, threw the rest in the toilet, then within seconds collapsed into convulsions. He went into a coma, from which, at this writing, he has not returned. Initial tests found strychnine in the blood, later ones did not. His wife branded the investigation into the case a whitewash.

The FBI was another agency that looked upon Intertel with some institutionalized suspicion, perhaps especially so when J. Edgar Hoover was at the tiller. Hoover was not enthralled with either Peloquin or Hundley, because they had criticized him and he could certainly hold a grudge.

In late 1970, not long after Intertel took on Hughes as a client, Peloquin sent Hoover a birthday note, joining "the legions of Americans who wish you a most happy birthday with many more to come." Peloquin received a reply from Hoover's secretary, Helen Gandy, thanking him for his thoughtfulness. However, she attached to her copy of the letter a mini-dossier on Peloquin, which noted: "Although the Bureau enjoyed favorable relations with Peloquin during the time he worked for the Department, he has since been critical of the Director of the FBI and on 1-29-69 he was quoted as saying the Director did not recognize the existence of organized crime until 1960 and it would be necessary for businessmen to 'harass' the FBI to get any results on organized crime matters."

Hoover was even more peeved at William Hundley. The dossier on Hundley at the FBI alleged that while at Justice, he mishandled the prosecution of a man named John J. Frank. He managed to get a conviction, but it was overturned on appeal. Upon hearing that Hundley had been maligning the FBI, Hoover told an underling, "If I recall correctly, he had the Frank case reversed on him because of errors he committed. He had better learn how to handle his own interests."

In 1962 Hundley received much press ink by dint of sitting with mob informant Joseph Valachi during his Senate testimony. Hundley was quoted in the press so often that Hoover was moved to exclaim, "Hundley certainly is a garrulous individual!"

And in 1966 the Boston *Globe* quoted Hundley to the effect that the FBI had taken up "bugging" in the early sixties because it had failed to develop an adequate intelligence system on organized crime. (Hundley was not alone in that belief.) The FBI refuted the statement, countering that they'd had an effective system in the forties. An assistant sent Hoover a memo detailing Hundley's quotes, and commented that "Hundley has also 'sold his soul.'" Hoover had the last word: "I would agree, if he ever had a soul."

At an FBI Executives Conference in 1971, Intertel was the topic of conversation. The word was passed that the Las Vegas FBI had been instructed to have nothing to do with the company. In 1972, when the Clifford Irving bogus Howard Hughes biography drama was unfolding, Intertel tried to coax a set of Hughes' fingerprints out of the FBI. Perhaps they were beginning to wonder if it was, in fact, Hughes they had in their care. The FBI denied the request for the prints. In 1978, when Resorts International was trying to get a casino license in New Jersey, they claimed that the FBI had once investigated them and given them a clean bill of health. The FBI instructed all of its branches to refuse to acknowledge any such clean bill.

But if Intertel-FBI relations were not always marked by cooperation, Intertel did exhibit some concern for its image in the FBI's eyes. When publisher Hank Greenspun's Las Vegas *Sun* ran a series of articles in 1971 calling Intertel a dangerous, mob-connected secret police force, Intertel reacted by putting together a voluminous rebuttal and shipping it off to the FBI. In 1972, when ABC News implicated Intertel in the ITT-Dita Beard scandal, Intertel quickly called the FBI to assure them it had nothing to do with Dita Beard. The FBI, however, noted that Intertel had done some work for ITT in connection with the case.

Ironically, despite all of the controversies that swirl around Intertel, despite its claims that it is guardian of airports and cities and conglomerates, Intertel is just one more of those Resorts subsidiaries that have trouble making ends meet. It has never been particularly profitable—though no doubt it has other value to Resorts.

CHAPTER EIGHTEEN

For all of its concern about its public image, Intertel's name might have been besmirched if details of the Hughes encampment came out. It was greatly romanticized, that Hughes move from Las Vegas to Paradise Island. Rumors about the man's health had been bandied about for years, but in the public consciousness he was still a sort of poetic, if reclusive, figure. In the past he had been a dashing aviator and businessman, involved with beautiful actresses—all the things the public wanted him to be. Now people wondered if it was true his fingernails were inches long and his hair streaming long too. The world that tried to peer through those ninth-floor windows saw only the sun reflecting back at them. Howard Hughes remained an almost mythical figure, a man who came and went with little interference from worldly cares, a man who could control his own destiny.

It wasn't true. Howard Hughes spent his days in Paradise in bed mostly, or if not in bed, walking naked about his room, emaciated, often in a stupor, prisoner of an addiction to codeine of decades' duration. One of the considerations in moving him from Las Vegas was to get him near an adequate supply of drugs. Another motive must have been to find a resting place to which he could be brought with the utmost discretion and where the strange night moves could be made with the minimum of bureaucratic hassle. What better place than Paradise Island? Customs and Immigration were docile—years of payoffs and Sy Alter's attentiveness had seen to that.

But Hughes' stay was not destined to be a lengthy one. One published version has it that Vesco was responsible for his sudden departure in early 1972. (Though others say Pindling didn't want to be embarrassed by Hughes in an election year.) The financier found a Bahamian law requiring alien island residents to have pictures on file, goes the story, and arranged for some camera-bearing government men to show up on the doorstep of the hysterically camera-shy Hughes. The cameramen scuffled with Hughes aides, then were forced to leave but vowed to return. When they did, Hughes was gone.

The story may be apocryphal, but it's not implausible. Robert Vesco was very kind to Lynden Pindling, and Pindling may have been repaying the favors. A more mysterious puzzle is, What would Robert Vesco want with Paradise Island? Through 1972, when he was dickering for it, the island and its casino were facing some tough challenges. The government had taken to raising casino taxes dramatically. Then, too, in 1972 the Bahamas won their independence and became a commonwealth. Pindling was now Prime Minister, and he wasted little time making it known that he intended that the government own the casinos.

Robert Vesco was a shrewd—if dishonest—businessman, too shrewd to spend millions of dollars without some assurances on something that could be rendered all but worthless by government fiat. It may have been that he was banking on his well-managed relationship with the government, his years of palm-greasing. For whatever reasons, negotiations were held. Resorts International first admitted they were taking place in February 1972, but refused to say with whom, except that it was not Howard Hughes. In April Resorts announced that talks had collapsed because they could not agree on terms or price. But in September the company said talks were on, and gave only hints as to who the potential buyer might be. Rumors that it was Vesco were lent credence when two of his top executives visited Paradise Island.

Eventually terms began to filter out. A local newspaper, the Nassau *Guardian,* announced a deal: RESORTS CHAIRMAN SAYS VESCO TO BUY PARADISE ISLAND FOR $80 MILLION. Lots of islanders were under that same impression, but it was a while before Crosby would talk. What preceded his willingness to do so was the sky, in the form of the SEC, falling in on Robert Vesco.

On November 27, 1972, Vesco and forty-one other defendants were smacked with one of the biggest fraud suits in the history of money. They had allegedly looted Investors Overseas Services, a mutual-fund complex, of hundreds of millions—if not billions—of dollars. The following day, Resorts chairman Crosby gave an interview to *The Wall Street Journal,* in which he said that negotiations with Vesco *might* be halted by the SEC fraud suit. He said the parties were "reasonably close" to a meeting of the minds but that negotiations "certainly" would be affected if "we can't get legal opinions" about an agreement.

Then he talked terms. The bidders were Gilbert Straub and Richard Clay, executives of Vesco holdings and codefendants in the SEC suit. The purchase price was "more than $15 million" for "most" of Resorts International's Paradise Island properties. He said that the Vesco group would buy the bridge for substantially below its appraised value because "they said they wouldn't buy the rest unless they could buy the bridge at that price."

A day later, Crosby talked some more. He hoped that the phrase "more than $15 million" had not created confusion.

The proposed sale price for the casino, two hotels and other Bahamian property was, in fact, $58 million. And Raymond Gore, the Resorts financial vice-president, added that the price would not include the bridge. Crosby would keep that and Resorts would hold on to one big and one small hotel. They weren't saying which ones.

But it didn't matter. Much as Resorts must have wanted to follow through on the deal—it was a safe bet that when the government bought them out, it wouldn't match Vesco's offer —it became apparent that they might be accepting stolen money, which could thrust them into a tangle of lawsuits. The sale was dropped. Vesco later fled to Costa Rica, eventually returning to Nassau, and Resorts kept Paradise to itself.

But where was super-sleuth Intertel when all of this was going on? Resorts International went through months of negotiations with a man who at the same time was allegedly pulling off one of the all-time great swindles. For all its pedigree, was the watchdog napping? Peloquin told me that Intertel did investigate Vesco, and while no charges against him were pending, they were convinced that something was wrong. He claimed that the negotiations with Vesco were slowed because of the suspicions and, indeed, that the deal with Vesco would have gone through had it not been for Intertel. "I'm proud," he said, "of the way we handled that one."

Crosby said that no one was ever suspicious, and insisted that no one told him not to deal with Vesco. "Vesco became a bad man overnight," he said.

Even by the time the company executives testified at hearings in New Jersey in early 1979, they had not gotten their stories in agreement. One said they had no idea Vesco was in trouble. In fact, just a day or two before the suit was brought, company executives had visited the SEC and gotten no preview of the coming event. Another said that the talks had been halted before the SEC suit.

After the talks fell through, Crosby reflected that maybe it wasn't such a bad thing after all. He told *The Wall Street Journal:* "A change in the atmosphere in the Bahamas encourages us to be far more confident of the future. Perhaps it wouldn't be advantageous to sell. We've been through seven hard years on the islands."

CHAPTER NINETEEN

Huntington Hartford had been through more long, hard years on the island than anyone, but his were coming to a close. The scene was set for his ouster as early as 1968. Hartford had never gotten along well with the executives from Resorts. The Resorts people found him frustrating to deal with. Crosby thought Hartford was a pest, one more annoying detail of life on Paradise Island. He was always popping up when you least wanted him to and wondering things like, Couldn't those carpenters stop working on that hotel and come build my oversized Ping-Pong invention? Getting rid of him was not too difficult.

When Hartford sold Paradise Island to Mary Carter Paint, he lent it $2 million toward construction of the Britannia Beach Hotel. In 1968 Hartford and a financial adviser flew to Acapulco and met with Jack Davis to tackle that debt, among other topics. Resorts wanted to wipe it clean. Hartford needed money, but instead of cash, what he got in exchange for forgiving the debt was 150,000 shares of Resorts International Class A stock. At the time, the stock was selling at around $28 a share.

Hartford's shares were not registered with the SEC, which

meant he could not sell them through normal stockbroker channels. He would either have to wait until they were registered—a lengthy process that involved much filing of papers and programs and waiting for approval from the SEC—or arrange a private placement, which was tricky too. The fact that he could not readily convert his stock to cash made Hartford jittery. It was no secret that his financial footing was increasingly precarious.

Hartford asked Davis what would happen if he wanted to sell out. What if he needed money in a hurry? Resorts came up with a proposal. If they failed to register the shares with the SEC within one year of the transaction date, they would arrange a million-dollar bank loan to the millionaire, and they would guarantee and pay interest on it. Hartford accepted the proposal.

A year came and went without Resorts' registering the shares. (The SEC says they never tried.) By that time, the value on the American Stock Exchange had dropped to around $16 a share, which meant that on paper, Hartford was approximately $1.8 million poorer. It didn't seem to matter because, as promised, in October 1969 Resorts orchestrated the loan. It was from the Bank of Commerce, a New York-based bank that was a long-time associate of the company. Its chairman, Russell Weiss, was a close personal friend of James Crosby and a director of Unexcelled Chemical as well as of Intertel. The loan was a "demand" type, meaning the bank could call it at any time. That didn't seem to be a problem either, because Resorts was the unconditional guarantor. But just to make sure the loan was not called, Resorts, says Hartford, persuaded him to put up some collateral. He was reluctant, but finally put up, at Resorts' suggestion, nearly 150,000 shares of the Resorts Class A stock that he owned and the 17.6 percent interest he held in the Island Hotel Company, a Resorts subsidiary.

Shortly after, Resorts did manage to register a big batch of shares with the SEC, but Hartford's were not among them. The company explained, he said, that if they added his shares to the large amount already being dumped on the market, it would only further depress the stock price.

Hartford was in a bind. He could not force them to register the shares, yet he needed the cash. The value of his stock had declined by over $2 million while he sat helplessly by. Then came the biggest blow. In June of 1973, Resorts informed Hartford that it was removing its guarantee of the loan, effective August 1. Hartford was in a panic. There was no way he could put together enough cash to ward off what he knew would come next. He knew the bank would call the loan. So in July he went to court seeking an injunction barring Resorts from removing its guarantee and preventing the bank from selling his collateral. The injunction was granted.

In August the bank called the loan. By that time Resorts had registered the shares, but they were not in Hartford's possession, and even if they had been, they would not have been worth selling. Their value had plummeted to $3 a share, and in total they were not worth half the face value of the loan. On paper, Hartford was out almost $4 million.

He pursued his case and Resorts put up a lively defense, arguing that a man with Hartford's life style—"bizarre as it might be"—with servants and houses all over the world, could hardly be strapped for a mere million. Hartford countered that the financial times were difficult ones. He could never liquidate his properties by the August deadline without using fire-sale tactics and suffering enormous financial distress.

Months later, the injunctions Hartford had obtained were lifted, and Resorts and the Bank of Commerce were swift to act. In December 1973 Resorts made a tender offer for its own shares at $2.50 apiece. The Bank of Commerce immediately tendered all of the Hartford collateral stock. Then in the spring of 1974, the bank held an auction of Hartford's Island Hotel

Company interests. There was only one bidder—Resorts International. They bought out the Hartford property for $20,000 and then proceeded to value it on their own financial records at close to $800,000.

Hartford unleashed another lawsuit in New York State court in July of 1974. He named James Crosby, Resorts International and the Bank of Commerce as defendants. He accused them of squeezing him financially. He charged that Resorts' prior dealings with Robert Vesco had been a contrivance to cheat him out of his share of the island. He said Crosby had deprived Resorts of a corporate opportunity by allowing the bridge to be operated as a private company. He alleged a conspiracy between Resorts and the Bank of Commerce. He claimed that Resorts was skimming casino funds off the top and not reporting them, which not only cheated the IRS but cheated him as well, because they had agreed that he would get a share of casino profits over a certain amount. He said that more than $26 million worth of expenses that were accumulated by other subsidiaries had been charged to the Paradise Island Limited subsidiary, and that Resorts refused to account for the expenses.

But he sued to no avail, because he ran out of funds and Resorts outlasted him. He was forced to settle out of court in October of 1974. For all of the time, effort and money he had put into Paradise Island—he claims he had spent more than $30 million—he got $1 million.

Resorts International got Hartford's property and a future unfettered by the pesky millionaire. He signed an agreement that he would never sue them again. Only if he can prove fraud, which he has spent years trying to do, will that contract be nullified. Meanwhile, he has but one more financial disaster to show for it all.

A disinterested observer wonders how terms could have been so loose, contracts so fraught with loopholes, how Hartford

could have agreed to a demand loan. His tone, when he answers, is that of an aging flower child: "I was naïve. I had a
tendency to think more about what it would look like and not
enough about money. I didn't know anything about the stock
market. I would sign whatever pieces of paper my advisers put
in front of me. I thought Davis and Crosby were nice fellows.
The stupid thing about my life is that I have always trusted
people."

Once Hartford visited Crosby's house on Paradise Island, he
reminisces, a modern showplace built with company funds. He
wanted to discuss their financial differences and to sell his
share. They had discussed it from time to time—would again
in the midst of the lawsuits—but they could never agree on
price. On this particular day the men were on the terrace and
Crosby was engrossed in a favorite pastime—backgammon.
"I'll sell my share," Hartford recalls telling Crosby. "I'll get
out. How much will you give me?" Crosby never lifted his eyes
from the board. "A million dollars," he replied.

Another time, an angry Hartford confronted Crosby and
demanded to know why the bridge did not belong to the
company. Why did Crosby and a bunch of businessmen get to
reap the rewards? Crosby turned to him and snapped, "What
else have I got to live on but revenues from the bridge?" And
on still another occasion, says Hartford, Crosby told him not
to worry about the casino, because casinos didn't make money.

By 1974 that was all in the past. For Huntington Hartford,
Paradise was lost.

CHAPTER TWENTY

In 1973 Resorts International found itself in the awkward position of tangling with two governments at once. The company was used to feuding with government bodies. In the United States, it was regulatory agencies, like the SEC and the IRS. In the Bahamas, there had been go-rounds on issues like taxes and getting work permits for non-Bahamians. But 1973 was a culmination because that was the year the peculiar activities at the time of Watergate surfaced and also the year that the Pindling government announced that effective with the expiration of Resorts' casino license in December 1977, the government, "as a matter of policy," would own the casino.

First Watergate. Resorts could deny its connection until the sand turned green, but they were never totally convincing. Richard Nixon had been a sometime visitor to Paradise Island for years. He was there as early as 1962—when Hartford owned the island—after his unsuccessful run for governor of California. On that visit Nixon was morose, and even amateur comedian Sy Alter could not cheer him up. Later on, in 1968, Crosby and Nixon became acquainted, not through Hartford but through Bebe Rebozo, whom Crosby met through Sy Alter. Nixon and Crosby hit it off immediately.

Nixon did one of his better imitations of relaxation on Paradise Island. Photographic history has recorded a fit-looking, tanned and short-shorts–clad James Crosby touring Nixon around his tropical lair. The sun was beating, the heat white-hot, and Nixon sported a dark suit and tie.

In 1968, the same year they met, Crosby made a $100,000 donation to the Nixon campaign. It took the unusual form of thirty-four checks, thirty-three of them for $3,000 apiece, the last for $1,000. In 1972 Crosby made no contribution, even though he was reportedly asked to by Herbert Kalmbach, Nixon's lawyer. Crosby was reported to have said that he felt he had given enough. Investigators wondered if perhaps Resorts had given in some less direct way, perhaps connected to Sy Alter's meanderings between the island and the Key Biscayne Bank. It was a strange coincidence that people started noticing Alter's banking activities only around the fall of 1972, the time of the presidential election and, too, the time of the Watergate break-in. That was also when, according to an IRS informant, Alter made an emergency call to the captain of the Resorts yacht to pick him up at the Jockey Club and take him to see Rebozo and "the man."

There were a lot of other coincidences, too: We know that Jack Davis's roommate showed up, after a felony conviction in New York, as a trust officer at the Key Biscayne Bank, and claimed he got the job through the classified ads. Intertel worked for ITT. Vesco negotiated, in 1972, to buy Paradise Island, at around the same time Resorts was trying to get Hartford out of it. Furthermore, Donald Nixon, the President's nephew, showed up on the payroll of a Vesco company.

It all led to avalanches of speculation. Were Resorts and Vesco involved in something together? Was Nixon laundering funds through the Paradise Island Casino to conceal their source? Was money from the casino being used to replace

funds that had left the election account at the Florida bank—
and shouldn't have—and had to be replaced in case investigators checked? There were countless questions like that. Many
of them will probably never be answered, but they are too
intriguing to go away.

CHAPTER TWENTY-ONE

As for the Bahamas, to hear David Probinsky tell the story, he alone was responsible for saving Resorts International's hide in those islands. He remembers the sequence of events as follows: When Probinsky signed his contract to do PR for Resorts, Jack Davis made a joke out of it. Probinsky's partners were all government officials, and Davis, tongue in cheek, said he guessed he had to sign because here were "all of these Bahamian politicians standing around and what the hell do you do?" They were to be paid $3,000 a month to handle minor duties, because a New York PR firm, Interpublic, was doing the important work.

A couple of years later, Davis fired Probinsky and discontinued the account, but the business relationship was reestablished years later, at about the time Crosby came to the islands, says Probinsky.

According to Probinsky (though, it must be noted, some islanders dispute it), Crosby had not spent much time on Paradise Island, instead overseeing operations from New York. Then in 1973, he came down to the island and announced that from now on, he was going to be making the decisions. The problem was that Davis had badly alienated the Progressive

Liberal party. The Prime Minister told Probinsky that he didn't trust the people at Paradise Island because he thought they still had allegiances to the prior white administration.

Crosby traveled south and surveyed the mess, and though he apparently didn't accuse anyone, Probinsky said it was pretty plain he blamed Jack Davis for botching things up. Crosby called Probinsky to his office and said, "You know, David, I'd like you to help me in any way you can." Crosby explained that at the time he was active in about ten public companies on the New York and American Stock Exchanges but that he had never had any dealings with black politicians. The fact that they were black politicians in a foreign country made it more confusing. He asked the PR man to fill him in on what made them tick, what they wanted, who was responsible for what.

So for days that is what Probinsky did: "I talked about it. I explained Mr. Pindling. I explained the political philosophy, as I understood it, was a part of the PLP. I explained what the objectives, as I knew them, were of the PLP. I explained . . . who were the good guys and who were the bad guys, meaning the political people." Probinsky told Crosby that there should be no doubt about the government's intentions— Pindling had spelled them out years earlier in the "bend or break" speech. Crosby asked Probinsky to intercede on the company's behalf.

Probinsky told Lynden Pindling the problem and assured him that Crosby was sincere and wanted to be friends. Relations improved, though never got to the point where the government felt comfortable about the executives across the channel. A solution was arrived at whereby Resorts was allowed to operate the casino, and eventually the one on Freeport as well, on terms that allowed it to prosper. Eventually, Pindling even invited Crosby to some kind of formal dinner at his house, which, as Probinsky put it, he was "not famous for doing."

Probinsky also gives himself credit for Resorts' interest in

Atlantic City. He claims he brought it to their attention in 1976, but that assertion has been challenged. Jack Davis and an Intertel executive testified in favor of gambling in New Jersey, and specifically Atlantic City, as early as 1970. Also in 1970, Resorts took a lease on two huge old hotels in Spring Lake, New Jersey. The company later denied they did so with casinos in mind (and they gave up the leases within a year), but some who knew them claim otherwise. As to New Jersey contacts who might clue them in on any pro-casino movements, there was State Senator Frank McDermott, a friend and neighbor of Resorts vice-president Raymond Gore in Summit, New Jersey. McDermott was very active in the push for casinos. Then, too, Henry Murphy, who was on the board of directors of Resorts International, was a resident of Trenton (the state capital of New Jersey), head of the local chamber of commerce and active in New Jersey affairs.

This is not to imply that Probinsky did not also have ties to New Jersey. He kept in touch with friends from his old neighborhood, and it was two old buddies, he says, who filled him in, in 1976, on what was going on. Probinsky was in the Bird Cage Lounge on Paradise Island one day with a man named Fulginetti and another named Zaberer, who owned a famous Atlantic City restaurant. The men told Probinsky there was a rumor that the casino issue was going to come up again. They told him he ought to find out about it, it might prove worthwhile.

That evening, says Probinsky, he called his old friend Marvin Perskie, a New Jersey lawyer, an influential lobbyist and the uncle of State Assemblyman Steven Perskie. Probinsky says he asked Marvin about the rumors, and Marvin told him they were true. As it happened, nephew Steve was sponsoring a bill to put a referendum on the November ballot. Probinsky decided it might warrant a trip to Atlantic City to see for himself. Maybe Resorts would be interested in knowing what it was all about.

The next day, Probinsky discussed the trip with Jack Davis. Davis said he had heard something about Atlantic City gambling already, that Bob Peloquin or Intertel or someone had checked it out, but they were not encouraged. But Davis said he would talk to Jim Crosby and get back to Probinsky. A day later, he agreed that Probinsky could go to Atlantic City, and a $2,000 expense account was authorized.

In Atlantic City, Probinsky met with Marvin Perskie, but the lawyer didn't have much time for him because he was in the middle of trying a case. He referred the PR man to his nephew the assemblyman. The nephew was helpful, told Probinsky where the referendum stood, what its chances were, and Probinsky was optimistic. He reported back to Paradise Island that this thing might work out. Crosby told him to go back again, get all the data he could—marketing information, airline schedules, traffic flows, tax ratables. Probinsky returned to Atlantic City and hired an airplane to take aerial photographs of the hotels while he looked into the political situation. He sent Crosby boxes of information that he thought would be meaningful, and he told the chairman that he really should come look for himself.

Crosby said he would, and he would bring Peloquin and Davis and a couple of others. Probinsky told Assemblyman Perskie that the brass was coming, and asked Perskie to arrange a proper welcome, set them up with real estate people and politicians and perhaps somebody from the Atlantic City Housing and Redevelopment Authority. Steve made all of the important contacts and even called the police, so that by the time the contingent from the Bahamas arrived, it had been arranged that they would ride in a caravan of limousines up and down the Boardwalk, inspecting the various hotels and piers. Later they would meet with the most influential politicians, including State Senator Joseph McGahn, who was the senate sponsor of the casino legislation.

Resorts didn't waste much time stacking its deck once it had an inkling this might be a good bet after all. It was not interested in petty politicians, in people who could not pull strings, could not weave with dexterity through the inroads and outroads of Trenton. It immediately signed up two lawyers—Marvin Perskie, the aforementioned uncle of Assemblyman Steve Perskie, and Pat McGahn, the brother of State Senator Joe McGahn. The lawyers were promised $35,000 apiece through the referendum—in other words, for six months' worth of consulting.

Resorts then managed to pick up an option on a fifty-five-acre Boardwalk-front tract of land from the Atlantic City Housing and Redevelopment Authority, even though it had already been optioned to a Philadelphia company. (The Philadelphia concern sued and it was later settled out of court. An HRA official later left the agency and entered into some land deals with Resorts' executives.) Resorts commissioned a poll to get voter reaction to the casino proposal, and when the results were favorable, they bought the Chalfonte-Haddon Hall Hotel, its glory days long gone but, it turned out, the most likely early casino candidate. They optioned a lot of other property. To protect the investment, they poured hundreds of thousands of dollars into a pro-casino lobby—the Committee to Rebuild Atlantic City—and other efforts to promote passage of the referendum.

The opposition could muster only a fraction of that amount. Nobody makes big bucks when casinos are turned down. If anti-casino forces spend a lot of money promoting against casinos, they have no way of recovering the money. It is the side that gets them in—namely the casino operators—who stands to gain financially.

The opposition was nevertheless impressive. The Council of Churches was dead set against casinos and said so often. (One Catholic parish was conspicuous in its refusal to come out against casinos. After the referendum passed, Resorts took some marshland off its hands. Neither party would disclose the price.) Law enforcement people were vocal too. U.S. Attorney Jonathan Goldstein was fervent on the subject. Attorney General William Hyland had been outspokenly anti-casino for years. When the issue arose in 1971, he presented testimony to a New Jersey senate committee on the ultimate effect casinos would have. He feared that organized crime would stampede in and undo all the progress New Jersey had made in fighting crime in recent years and in changing its mob-haven image. Hyland was all but ridiculed by the committee head, State Senator Frank McDermott (the Union County neighbor of Resorts V.P. Gore). Was the state's highest law enforcement official saying that he was not capable of controlling crime? Was he saying that his office was inept?

In 1976, crusading law enforcement officials and clergymen and legions of just plain folk were no match for the pro-casino forces (who did number in their ranks, incidentally, at least one law enforcement official: Joseph Lordi, Essex County prosecutor). The Committee to Rebuild Atlantic City got people like Danny Thomas and Peggy Lee to stage fun benefits for casino gambling. Their advertising was slicker; their public relations campaign was mounted by a skilled California media man, Sanford Weiner. And minorities were appealed to over and over again. All of that was the reason why overnight, in November 1976, thanks to some well-timed real estate purchases, Resorts International was an immensely richer company. And David Probinsky would be immensely richer too.

CHAPTER TWENTY-TWO

David Probinsky didn't feel secure in his job and he wanted a contract. He had wanted one since early in his relations with Resorts so he would be certain to get what he deserved for all of the good will he had drummed up between Paradise Island and the Bahamian government, and also because he was not getting along with some of the people at Resorts International, notably Davis and Peloquin. He was afraid that would cost him his job.

But it took years to get a contract, until 1976, in fact, after he had introduced Resorts to Atlantic City. One day at Paradise Island, Probinsky stormed into the executive offices and began to rant; no one could understand him. So he told them, "I am talking about some protection as far as my involvement here in the Bahamas for the last years, and if something develops in Atlantic City, I want something in writing." Crosby told him, "It's not the policy of the company to have anything in writing." But, he added, "Let's see what you have in mind. Let's talk about it and see what develops."

What developed was an agreement between Resorts International and David Probinsky, dated July 1, 1976. The contract noted that Probinsky had performed public relations work for

Resorts in the past, and that the parties desired to "resolve certain matters presently existing between them." It declared that Resorts was interested in the renewal of its Paradise Island operating license, wanted "the support and assistance of Probinsky and is prepared to remunerate Probinsky in this connection on a contingency basis only."

Under paragraph 1 of the contract, Probinsky was to be paid at a yearly rate of $40,000 in equal installments for eighteen months, starting with the date of the contract—for a total of $60,000. Under paragraph 2, he would receive—contingent on Resorts' being allowed to continue running the Paradise Island Casino—$30,000 a year for ten years or as long as Resorts operated that casino, plus an option to purchase 12,500 shares of Resorts Class A stock. Under paragraph 3, he would receive, contingent on Resorts' getting a license in Atlantic City, $35,000 a year for ten years or as long as Resorts operated in Atlantic City. And he got another four-year option to purchase Class A common shares. In other words, before options— which would eventually push the value of the contract well into the millions—the contract was potentially worth $710,000 to Probinsky. But there were conditions that made it seem as if Probinsky was being paid not only for his valuable services, past and present, but to, in effect, get out of town and stay out. Resorts made it clear it did not want David Probinsky around and talking.

First, Probinsky had to agree to "remove himself from the State of New Jersey and not to have any contact directly or indirectly therein during the term of this agreement or until the corporation shall have determined not to pursue its objectives therein whichever shall first occur."

Probinsky further had to agree to take no action of any kind "inimical to the best interests of the corporation." And he had to agree that he would not utter any statement critical of the corporation. More humorous was a clause that read that when requested by the company, Probinsky would have to embark on business trips to Europe and Central and South America, and "in connection therewith to immediately undertake a trip to the south of France for the purpose of exploring business opportunities of possible interest to the corporation." Probinsky was provided with two round-trip, first-class tickets.

All the parties agreed to keep the contract in the strictest secrecy. Immediately after signing, Probinsky vacated a house he had been renting in Margate, New Jersey, and took off.

In late 1977, Resorts had not yet received a license in Atlantic City, and it claimed it could not predict the outcome of its license negotiations with the Bahamian government, even though the license expired in December. At Christmas time, Larry Rice, a Resorts financial executive, called Probinsky in Mexico, where he was spending the holidays, and told him that as of January 1, his contract was up. He said there was nothing the company could do about it, except maybe give Probinsky $40,000 or $50,000. Probinsky slammed the phone down, furious. He called Crosby in Nassau and recounted what had happened. Crosby told him to calm down, they would discuss it, and he agreed to meet Probinsky at the Jockey Club in Miami. But in May of 1978, Probinsky still did not have a contract. And May of 1978 was exactly the time that investigators in New Jersey were trying to find out what various people, Probinsky among them, knew about Resorts International.

Probinsky called his New Jersey lawyer, George James, and told him that unless the contract was renewed, he was going to sue. Furthermore, he said, he was sick and tired of hearing from all of his friends in Wildwood that he was hiding out in Israel, that he was "up some back alley." He told the lawyer to call the gaming commission and tell them, "David Probinsky is ready to meet with them and do any damn thing they want." George James relayed the message, said Probinsky, but by the time anyone got around to calling back, it was November, and by November Probinsky wasn't angry anymore. He had a new contract.

The terms were similar to the first, and once again he promised to maintain his silence and leave the country. The contract would, due in large part to the stock options, turn out to be worth millions of dollars.

After it was signed, Probinsky got a call from Marvin Perskie, whom by that time Probinsky was also not getting along with. According to him, Perskie said, "You've got five days to leave Atlantic City. The company needs the house you are living in." Probinsky was livid, but Perskie's wife cooled him down and persuaded him to leave. She told him he was "only rocking boats." Probinsky left town and Resorts did not have to worry about him anymore—until the next contract, that is.

In the meantime, Resorts could go about its multimillion-winning ways and hit the biggest jackpots it had ever won. One on the American Stock Exchange, the other in Atlantic City.

PART THREE

THE FALL OF NEW JERSEY

CHAPTER TWENTY-THREE

Atlantic City, New Jersey, is not the place where one would expect to fulfill one's wildest expectations. In 1977 it could not have been particularly inspiring to executives schooled in the board rooms of Park Avenue or spoiled by life in Paradise. There was not much to do that was sophisticated. There were a few good restaurants, like the Knife and Fork and the Palm Court over at the Howard Johnson's, but there was not the jazzy night life of New York City, the sort an urban corporate player might be used to. Atlantic City was a dull gray town, almost three hours' drive from New York, and Jack Davis, for one, was quick to admit he really couldn't stand the place.

Still, he had to be there, and in Trenton, at times, and so did James Crosby on occasion and Steve Norton and lawyer Charlie Murphy. They had to be on the spot almost as soon as the referendum was passed, because within days bills would be proposed to set up the ground rules and Resorts had a big investment to watch out for.

Helping them were the two well-connected lawyers, Perskie and McGahn. There had been bills kicking around the State-house since before the referendum, and their sponsors were quick to try to push them through. The senate and assembly bills were almost identical, and the sponsors were, in the senate, Joe McGahn, and in the assembly, Steven Perskie.

If lawyers Perskie and McGahn were not protection enough for Resorts' investment, they hired another one. He was Joel Sterns, a jolly roundish man with a walrus mustache who was well read and well liked, could talk opera and theater and sports. More important, he was one of the premier lobbyists in Trenton. He was the former counsel to once Governor, later State Supreme Court Chief Justice Richard J. Hughes. (When Hughes stepped down from the chief justice's bench in 1979, he joined the Sterns law firm.) Sterns was also counsel to "Democrats for Byrne" in Brendan Byrne's successful gubernatorial campaign.

With all of that legal talent, corporate citizen Resorts did not have much trouble staying close to the situation in the caucus rooms of Trenton. Its influence was quickly felt. Tom Hester, a reporter from New Jersey's *Daily Home News,* called the making of the Casino Control Act a lesson in civics the likes of which none of the reporters covering it had ever received in high school.

Only days after New Jersey U.S. Attorney Jonathan Goldstein blasted the McGahn-Perskie proposals as "the child of special interests who hope to reap tens of millions of dollars in profits at the expense of our working citizens," State Senator McGahn urged an amendment to the bill that would increase the required minimum number of rooms in a casino hotel from four hundred to seven hundred and fifty. McGahn said he wanted to encourage construction, but sharp-eyed reporters were quick to point out that four hundred rooms would have made several hotels eligible for an early opening; with the higher requirement, the only hotel that qualified was the Chalfonte-Haddon Hall, owned by Resorts International. McGahn's blatant move spurred Brendan Byrne to comment that "if somebody submits a regulation which favors seven hundred and fifty rooms, you've got to look and see if he represents someone holding seven hundred and fifty rooms."

Legislators worried over other issues, like what the headlines liked to call "booze, bets and tips." Should casinos be allowed to serve liquor? they wondered. The argument against was that drinking lowered resistance to betting over one's head. The final bill allowed liquor. These may have seemed small points, but they were important to casino executives, who knew the psychology of gambling and how to make more money with more drinks and longer hours and higher minimum bets.

The casinos got pretty much what they wanted. The assembly State Government Committee created the Casino Control Act after five sessions dominated by Resorts International. Resorts president Jack Davis made it to all the sessions, as did lawyers Joel Sterns and Charlie Murphy. By late in the fourth session, Murphy was sitting at the committee table with the special assistant to the attorney general, Robert Martinez, a penner of the bill, trying to win points for his team.

Reporter Tom Hester wrote that a casino gambling report put out by the State Commission of Investigation (it had been requested by the governor) was brushed aside on the excuse that it had arrived late. And Hester noticed that while "young SCI attorney Jay Huntedtmark, who was no match for the casino pros, was urging sixteen-hour-a-day casino operations . . . behind his back Resorts attorney Pat McGahn made a choking gesture with a fist, signaling his brother, Sen. Joseph McGahn . . . at the committee table to cut him off. Senator McGahn quickly interrupted Huntedtmark and changed the subject." (Senator McGahn, a physician, later lost his senate seat and showed up as house doctor at Resorts.)

On another day, Hester reported, as the committee was about to reconvene for the afternoon session, Assemblyman Steve Perskie turned to Resorts executive Steve Norton and said, "Get the boys." Norton hurried to a phone and summoned Davis and Sterns back to the Statehouse.

The State Commission of Investigation and the attorney general's office were supposed to constitute a strong front against an overpowering casino lobby, but the front quickly caved in, and when the assembly passed its bill in April of 1977, casino operators didn't have much to complain about.

So it was on to the senate and more of the same. Senators, too, worried about easy casino credit and hours and liquor, but in the end casino credit was easy and liquor was free of charge and free-flowing, tips were allowed and casinos would operate eighteen hours daily and twenty hours on weekends. Also, when all the machinations were through, the minimum room count would have been lowered from the McGahn proposal but upped from the original four hundred to five hundred, and Resorts International would still have the advantage. When all the legislative brouhaha was through with one stroke of the governor's pen, the Resorts International Hotel would still be the only one to qualify, with a minimum of time and expense, to open a casino quickly. The stroke of the pen would be worth a fortune to Resorts International.

Resorts' influence may have surfaced in other aspects of the legislation. Long gone, for example, was an early proposal that no casino could open until at least three were ready. And there was another provision that was interesting in its omission. This northeast state had been boasting that it was enacting legislation not only with teeth but with jaws. The law was patterned after Nevada's, but it was stronger, the state said. It paid more heed to scrupulously investigating ancillary services, for example. Why, then, some who read it might wonder, did it omit the clause Nevada felt so strongly about? The one that said if you operate in Nevada, you can't operate elsewhere. Nevada would later knuckle under to the pressure of casinos wanting to go to Atlantic City, and would pass a new law allowing the operators to go to areas whose standards lived up to the alleged standards of Nevada. But even then Resorts International would not have been eligible, because it was doubtful the casino regulations of the Bahamas would pass Nevada muster. The company would not face that problem in New Jersey, though, because even though the eastern state had patterned its casino laws after those in Nevada, that one provision had somehow slipped by.

On June 2, 1977, the day that Brendan Byrne was to sign the casino legislation, there may have been more action on the Boardwalk than in the last ten years put together. Everybody said it looked just like the good old days. Thousands of people were there, civic workers and high school students were given a holiday, and there were marching bands and clowns and tap-dancing kids in yellow sequins. The politicians came out in droves from all over New Jersey. It was an election year, and at times the festivities and speeches were all but drowned out by the planes that droned overhead trailing streamers that encouraged votes for candidates named Byrne and Zold and Roe. Candidate Bateman was represented by a big blimp-type balloon borrowed from a neighboring amusement park.

The governor rode the long planking in an open convertible, sitting atop the back seat, waving, grinning, shaking hands. The band was playing "Happy Days Are Here Again" and Byrne supporters handed out leaflets while, pulling up the rear, others handed out all manner of posters and papers supporting his opponents.

Further in the background were lots of sticky little New Jersey politics about who was going to get to introduce the governor. The governor wanted Steve Perskie, and he said if he couldn't have Steve Perskie, he was going to take his little ceremony and move it right straight up to Trenton instead of Atlantic City. That worried Atlantic City Mayor Joseph Lazarow into giving the governor his way instead of introducing him himself or perhaps giving the honor to Senator Joe McGahn.

Byrne was angry because, while Perskie had endorsed him in his bid for reelection, McGahn had not. Also, Perskie was running for McGahn's senate seat, which made those two new enemies. When it came time for the introduction, Perskie got the honor and was accompanied by a drum roll. Poor McGahn got to say a few words, but he didn't get a drum roll and he didn't get to sit next to the governor, like Perskie did.

Then came the signing and with it the most dramatic speech of Byrne's career, an attempt at charisma in a delivery which was awfully reminiscent of a speech given years earlier by a Nevada governor. Byrne raised his fist to the sky on this "historic" occasion, and with throbbing voice proclaimed: "Organized crime is not welcome in Atlantic City! And we warn them again: Keep your filthy hands out of Atlantic City and keep the hell out of our state!"

Organized crime must have gotten a chuckle out of that one. They had been laying tracks for years and it would take more than the likes of Brendan Byrne to keep them out.

CHAPTER TWENTY-FOUR

On an autumn morning in 1977, Dennis Gomes and his wife and two children packed into a compact car and headed east from Nevada. Their destination was New Jersey, where Dennis had accepted a new job. Gomes was an accountant by training, an investigator by profession. He was leaving a position as chief of the audit division of the Nevada Gaming Control Board to take a similar one as head of the Special Investigations Bureau of the New Jersey Division of Gaming Enforcement. He was a soft-spoken man with dark hair, glasses, the slim build of a runner and a reputation as an untouchable. He was not inclined toward compromise. To a lot of people, many of them in the press, he was a hero. To the casino industry, he was something else. On being told of Gomes' move east, one casino executive reportedly said, "I hope the plane crashes."

The comment was all but a tribute to Gomes. A new-day law enforcer, he was skilled in following a dollar, in seeing where procedures were lax and what that could mean, in detecting a skim. To tell the story of how Dennis Gomes came to be going to New Jersey is to back up and tell the story of how gambling began in Las Vegas and how it evolved, because Dennis Gomes was an important part of that evolution.

Nevada was still a territory a hundred years ago when gambling first became a common pastime there—presumably because cowboys and prospectors couldn't find much else to do with their desert nights. Through the 1860s, Nevada flirted on and off with bills to outlaw the activity, but they never stuck, and in 1869—Nevada by then a state—gambling halls were legalized over the governor's veto. A quarterly fee was slapped on the activity and gambling was restricted to the "back room" —two provisions which were expected to deter a lot of the activity without outlawing it. But it takes an awful lot of heavy fee-slapping to dissuade a casino operator, since he knows that by continuing to operate, he can earn the money back in spades. As for the clause about back rooms, it had little effect except to supply a lot of cowboy-show writers, years later, with lines. The swinging doors fly open, in struts Wyatt Earp demanding to know where Bad Bart is. Bad Bart was always in the back room, dealing a few with the boys.

As the gambling business thrived, the stakes got larger and the treachery increased—the cheating by both house and player. The "skim" was born—taking money off the top and failing to report it. Nevada's response was to pass a bill, in 1879, outlawing cheating.

In 1909, as a new wave of Puritanism engulfed the country, Nevada outlawed gambling. The effect was to push the back room underground. By then there were far too many operators who were up on which politicians were ripe for a bribe and what sheriff would look the other way. Business went on more or less as usual (though over the years the law was occasionally relaxed and occasionally strengthened), and in the early 1930s, gambling was once again legalized.

In the forties William Harrah opened an establishment in Reno and later one in Lake Tahoe. Harrah wanted to give gambling a good name, and he did—his own. His casinos still bear his name, though control has recently been relinquished to Holiday Inn. Harrah's is one of the few casino operations that has maintained a straight-shooter reputation through the years. Others, like Benjamin "Bugsy" Siegel, who might be described as the father of modern Las Vegas, were not as interested in such reputations.

In the late forties, Bugsy was thrown out of California for illegal gambling operations, including book-making and running offshore casinos. He fled to Nevada, a state that looked on such activities with somewhat more favor. Bugsy hailed from the east, where he numbered among his friends the likes of Meyer Lansky and Lucky Luciano. Siegel was said to be a member of the notorious Murder Inc. His background was no secret in Nevada, but it was ignored because Bugsy was big time. He stood for progress, he had lots of money he was willing to spend and he knew how to run a gambling operation. The Flamingo Hotel, the first of the major neon-spackled hotel-casinos to go up on "the Strip," was built by Bugsy. He filled it with plush rooms and fancy restaurants, and invented the extravagant shows with big-name talent.

For his friends in the mob, he performed an invaluable service, supplying them with a lucrative new hobby. They helped him along in the beginning, seeing to it that he got supplies that were scarce during the war. But in 1947 Bugsy was murdered, execution style, in the Beverly Hills home of his mistress. His friends thought he was doing them dirty, skimming off the top of construction funds. Bugsy never got to see his ultimate dream come to fruition, his neon netherworld in the desert.

The Bugsy breach was quickly filled by other men with questionable pasts but grand plans, and Las Vegas bloomed in the desert, springing up almost overnight. It was an unwieldy growth that defied efforts to police it. In 1955 the first Nevada

Tax Commission was organized to make sure the state got its share of the take. It was a big job because the people who were running the casinos were a lot more adept at hiding money than the enforcers were at finding it. Furthermore, the folks who by then were responsible for establishments like the Flamingo, the Desert Inn, the Sands, the Dunes and the Sahara were of questionable background, but they were also the life-blood of Nevada industry and the center of Nevada society. They had created a gimmick to lure Californians across the border and send them back poorer. How could the state throw them out? It really didn't want to, so despite all the nifty new rules and regulations being set up to weed out the good guys from the bad, the mob was "grandfathered" in—they were allowed to stay because they were already there.

Las Vegas was a hundred-million-dollar cash machine—one day to be a billion—and a lot of that cash was in the hands of men who had only the most dishonorable intentions. They were men who would think nothing of bribing a senator or a congressman or anyone else who might prove useful. People outside the state worried that with all of that money, the casinos' influence would extend far beyond the borders of Nevada. The question of how far was never answered.

One of the people who grappled with it was Senator Estes Kefauver, whose Senate committee hearings into organized crime in interstate commerce in the early fifties led him to, among other places, Las Vegas. The Kefauver committee was incredulous to learn during its investigation that one of the first moves of the Nevada Tax Commission was to license the hoodlums who had been hanging around for years, many of whom had been convicted of felonies. The Kefauver hearings stirred up enough outside interest in Nevada that gangsters began to realize that in time law enforcement bodies might get serious about throwing them out. So they did the authorities a favor and returned to the "back room" in a figurative sense.

What authorities would now have to worry about were "hidden interests." When Frank Costello was murdered in New York in 1957, for example, there were papers in his pocket detailing gaming revenues from the Tropicana Hotel in Las Vegas, the implication being that he had a hidden interest in that hotel.

In 1955 the tax commission tried to shut down the Thunderbird Hotel and Casino in Vegas, claiming that Jake and his brother Meyer Lansky had a piece of the action. They cited as evidence the fact that Jake had contributed a large sum to the construction of the hotel. The commission was slapped down by the Nevada Supreme Court, which asserted that since there was proof only that Lansky had contributed to the hotel construction, he could not be said to be directly participating in the operation of the casino.

The state moved to strengthen its hand in 1959, when it replaced the tax commission with the Nevada Gaming Commission, which had the power to bestow and revoke licenses. Whereas the governor had previously had direct control over licenses, he now removed himself from that position. But it was not taken out of the realm of politics: the governor still had a strong indirect control in that he appointed the commissioners and they made the decisions. The investigative arm of the new casino-control structure was the Nevada Gaming Control Board. They conducted the background checks, kept tabs on the casinos, presented findings and recommendations to the commission regarding fines and who should and should not be allowed a license. The commission then voted either to uphold or to deny the recommendations.

Despite all of those changes, Nevada made only small strides in its housecleaning, but the feds were still in the picture too. In 1960, when John Kennedy was elected President, he appointed his brother Robert to the post of attorney general and Bobby aimed his guns west, to Nevada. Kennedy was out to get organized crime and he saw Las Vegas as a stronghold of such hoodlumism. He thought that money from Las Vegas casinos was being used to fund crime activities throughout the country. He didn't make many friends in Nevada when his federal agents barnstormed through the state. Nevada felt picked on, especially so because of massive leaks to the press by Kennedy men.

Bobby Kennedy was also taking aim at Jimmy Hoffa, the notorious leader of the corruptly run Teamsters Union. The attorney general wanted to clean up the union's Central States Pension Fund, which was to organized crime and casinos what the tooth fairy was to little children.

Nevada authorities were no more enthralled with Kennedy's tactics than were the casino executives. He was telling the state enforcers that they were incapable of enforcing—or perhaps unwilling. At one point, Kennedy blueprinted a skim-seeking scheme, a gigantic simultaneous raid on almost all of the Las Vegas casinos. He was dissuaded by local officials. One tactic that he did use, and it surfaced only much later, was to wiretap the phones and bug the offices of casino executives. The government was never able to use the taps as evidence in court proceedings because they were illegal under Nevada law, but to this day, names and events overheard are used as a reference point by investigators seeking to know who is tied to whom in crime circles.

Nevada and its governor, Grant Sawyer, were livid. They accused the FBI of violating the rights of Nevada citizens. What probably made them even angrier was the slap in the face state regulators had taken and the humiliation they suffered in the press. The Justice Department was telling Nevada that it had better do something to clean up the state or it could expect the law to continue breathing down its neck. In the late sixties, Nevada decided it was time to legitimize the state in the eyes of not only the federal government and the rest of the country but also, and perhaps most important, investors and the public companies who more and more were showing an interest in gambling casinos. It was with that "get-tough" attitude in mind that Nevada hired investigators like Dennis Gomes.

Gomes was a twenty-seven-year-old C.P.A. in 1971 when he joined the Nevada Gaming Control Board as chief of the audit division. In those days the division had only fifteen investigators and concerned itself mostly with tax violations. By 1977 Gomes had piloted it into a sixty-man team grappling with everything from background checks on casino executives to audits of the casinos themselves.

But even with forces like that, policing casinos is an awesome task. There are too many scams going on from too many different directions. The mob has increasingly taken to claiming it got its hands on enormous amounts of money—in actuality, for example, drug money—by winning it at the tables in Vegas. It is all but impossible for state and federal investigators to prove otherwise. Then there are the employee rip-offs of the casinos and there are casino skims of their own operations.

Still, if there was a enforcer likely to make a dent, it was Dennis Gomes. In 1976, for example, acting on a tip from informants (and after two raids made by his men had uncovered nothing), Gomes led a crew of investigators on an evening raid of the counting room of the Stardust Casino. The result was a several-hundred-page report alleging that employees of the casino were engaged in a $7 million skim of the slot machines at three casinos, all of them controlled by Argent Corporation. Argent, in turn, was controlled by Allen Glick, a man who had gone from being an $800-a-week salesman in California to a multimillion-dollar casino czar in just five years, thanks to over $100 million of loans from Teamsters pension funds. The ease with which he borrowed vast amounts of money has led to continuing investigations into whether he is a front for the mob.

The supposed mastermind of the slot-machine skim was George Jay Vandermark, hired by Argent in November 1974, just two months after Glick took over. When Gomes and his men dropped in unexpectedly, they discovered thousands of dollars in quarters that hadn't been recorded on the books. They demanded the key to an area where they thought they might find more of the same, and an employee said that only Vandermark had the key. Another employee phoned Vandermark and told him that Gomes was threatening to drill through the door. Vandermark reportedly said, "Screw 'em, let them drill it open. It gives us more time."

Later Vandermark fled to Mexico under an assumed name. When officials learned he was there, they dispatched his twenty-seven-year-old son to tell him he could escape prosecution if he testified. Shortly after returning from Mexico, the son was found murdered in bed, his head crushed. His father took off for Costa Rica, and the guess is that he, too, has been murdered because the mob feared he would talk.

The result of the Gomes disclosures was that the control board recommended Argent be fined nearly $12 million, but eventually it was fined just over $500,000.

The Stardust Casino's problems didn't end there. Allen Glick was eventually thrown out by the state, but his successor, Allan Sachs, is equally controversial. When his application was rammed through and given approval, one of the state's top gambling officials resigned in protest. And later, in 1979, thousands of dollars of bills were found in Stardust Casino money wrappers on a supected drug-smuggling plane in Florida. Investigators think money skimmed from the Stardust may be funding drug purchases in South America, as it is highly unusual for casino wrappers to be found outside a casino or its bank.

Gomes' methods were often flamboyant, which added to the white-knight-on-a-charger reputation he enjoyed in the press. He got results, but his recommendations and those of the gaming board were not always heeded. Some higher officials were less willing to alienate the all-powerful casino hierarchy. In a 1975 report by the board to the gaming commission, potentially big problems at the Aladdin Hotel and Casino were outlined. The hotel entertainment director had forty arrests and two felony convictions on his record. An alleged St. Louis racketeer was a guest of the hotel for three weeks and was advanced over $20,000 in credit. A former business partner of his worked at the Aladdin and took part in counting slot-machine take.

But the report was ignored by the Nevada commission, and the state was embarrassed when in 1979, four alleged organized-crime figures were convicted in a Detroit federal court of concealing their interests in the Aladdin hotel-casino. The judge in the case remarked that "the state of Nevada seems to be reluctant to prosecute offenses committed under its own laws."

After the Detroit convictions, there was little Nevada could do but revoke the Aladdin's operating license and order it sold. But the stream of potential buyers was no more savory than the evictees. It took several tries before buyers appeared who were more pleasing to regulatory souls. The first sign of hope was when National Kinney, a parking-garage company, announced that it would buy the Aladdin in partnership with entertainer Johnny Carson. But the SEC reportedly would slow that one down by scrutinizing Kinney filings, and besides, it eventually fell through for lack of financing.

In the papers the FBI filed in connection with the Aladdin trial, there are a host of hints that the Aladdin is far from alone in failing to report hidden interests. The FBI is also investigating, for example, the Tropicana because Carl DeLuna, an alleged big man in the Kansas City mob, is said to have a participation there. The papers also describe what look like attempts by the Kansas City mob to ensure that new owners of casinos meet with their approval, to manipulate stock and to influence top Nevada officials. They also reveal the existence of a recorded telephone conversation between Morris Shenker, principal shareholder in the Dunes Hotel-Casino, and Nicholas Civella, whom law enforcement sources believe to be the king-pin of the Kansas City mob. Shenker has long been under scrutiny by investigators in Nevada and at the federal level.

In 1979 the Del E. Webb Corporation, owner of the Sahara Hotel and Casino in Las Vegas (and, it hopes, in Atlantic City), was indicted on federal charges of conspiring to defraud the Teamsters Union Central States Pension Fund of a million dollars. That case is still pending.

One popular theory advanced over the years is that the increased entry of public companies into casinos has begun to make an honest state of Nevada. But the Dunes and Del E. Webb are both publicly held and so is Caesar's World, opera-tor of the glamorous Caesar's Palace, which was the subject of a 1976 Gomes report. Gomes recommended "strong discipli-nary action" against Caesar's—which could mean revoking its license—because the company had ignored a number of state warnings not to associate with certain people, including Alvin Malnik, the Miami lawyer. (Malnik, as noted, had dealings with Huntington Hartford and was the lawyer Sy Alter claimed introduced him to Meyer Lansky.) Gomes contended that since Caesar's management had chosen to ignore prior warn-ings, the company's continued operating presence in Nevada might damage the state's reputation. Gomes' recommenda-tions were not embraced; the company was simply warned once more.

In 1977 a new chairman, Harry Reid, was appointed to the gaming commission. A thirty-seven-year-old lawyer and former politician, Reid was almost immediately controversial. When the gaming board deemed the prospective buyer of the Haci-enda Hotel unsuitable, it was overruled by the commission.

Reid rubbed salt in the wound by publicly criticizing the board's investigation. In another action, Reid led the commission in approving an additional investor to the Tropicana Hotel whose application the board had voted down. Even some casino executives questioned the wisdom of Reid's moves, fearing that it would appear that Nevada was lowering its standards and would hurt their ability to raise capital.

At the gaming board, morale sunk to new depths and investigators began to seek employment elsewhere. A Nevada governor, Grant Sawyer, had once proclaimed (in the speech that Brendan Byrne of New Jersey would later echo eerily): "I agree with any measures to keep hoodlums out of Nevada. We might serve notice on underworld characters right now. They are not welcome in Nevada and we aren't going to have them here." But after a while, investigators started to think that the state hadn't really meant it at all.

Some investigators left the board and went to work in law firms, many of whose clients were casinos. Others went to work for the casinos themselves. Not Dennis Gomes. He loved law enforcement and he still believed in it. He thought it could work, but not in this particular state, at this particular time, under this particular commission chairman. And that is why when a man named Martinez came to call, Dennis Gomes was in a receptive frame of mind.

Robert P. Martinez was the newly appointed director of the Division of Gaming Enforcement in New Jersey, a bureau analogous to the Nevada Gaming Control Board. It was a title Martinez ascended to after paying his dues as a special assistant to New Jersey Attorney General William Hyland and after a stint as a principal architect of the casino-enabling legislation. Martinez was a big, burly, black-bearded man who had achieved some notoriety when he handled the reinvestigation into whether there was evidence that Bruno Hauptmann had *not* been the kidnapper-murderer of the Lindbergh baby. He got more publicity with his new appointment. The day after his swearing in, many of the New York, New Jersey and Philadelphia papers carried a picture of him kissing his wife over the head of his mother, who beamed approval upward.

While working on the gambling legislation, Martinez visited casinos in various parts of the world and, the attorney general said, "He learned more about the intricacies of casino gambling than anybody else in the state." But it wasn't enough. New Jersey needed the in-state services of someone who had not just studied casinos but had experience policing them. Martinez needed to know how to go about hiring an investigative team. He had to know who did what and which gambling procedures were preferable. It was an education starting at almost ground zero, and one of the teachers he asked to enlighten him was Dennis Gomes.

Gomes told him that gambling was a complicated business and it took sophisticated people to police it, people with good solid accounting backgrounds. You couldn't just throw in some rookie accountant who had been going over balance sheets at Price Waterhouse and expect him to catch a savvy cheat who skimmed by falsifying markers or figure out that the slot-machine change booth is being run in a way that encourages stealing. It took years of training to learn how to ferret those things out.

New Jersey knew from the start it would have to put Nevada enforcers on its payroll, and as a result of those meetings between Gomes and Martinez, Gomes was offered a job. Martinez painted a pretty picture: Gomes would be in charge of the Special Investigations Bureau of the Division of Gaming Enforcement. He would be paid an annual salary of $35,000 —more than half again what he earned in Nevada. Gomes would have the freedom to hire and fire whom he pleased, he would be allowed to build a staff of forty men and women, he would have a manageable budget, and he could run things as he saw fit, uninfluenced by governors or commissioners or anyone else. The Division of Gaming Enforcement would be part of the attorney general's office. Attorney General Hyland was outspokenly anti-casino and would thus encourage all efforts to keep the industry honest, would not try to stop investigations for political reasons.

Besides, New Jersey was a highly industrialized state and, unlike Nevada, would not rely on casinos for any meaningful contribution to revenues. Thus, the industry's influence would not be so strong that it would be able to curry undue favor.

Most appealing to Gomes, he would have the unprecedented luxury of starting a casino executive squad from scratch. These were exactly the kinds of conditions he would have liked to have had to work with in Nevada.

The problem for Gomes was New Jersey: it was best known for the New Jersey Turnpike, which wound past grimy, smoke-spewing factories that smelled so much you had to hold your nose going by. It called itself the Garden State, but everybody from everywhere knew what a joke that was. Then, too, Gomes' wife was a dancer. Las Vegas was a good place for her work, but New Jersey? Certainly not Trenton, where Dennis would be stationed. And it was too far from New York to think about dancing there. Atlantic City might be a possibility someday, but that was a long commute too. So though the job offer was tempting, New Jersey was not the Gomes' ideal state.

Martinez suggested they come look it over; maybe they could get used to it. They agreed that they could do that much.

The beginning of the drive from Newark Airport to Trenton is not auspicious. First there are the areas with the putrid factories and filth-caked terrain. Then, when you get off at Exit 9 and onto Route 1, the landscape has that unplanned look of highways everywhere in America: a flat, straight road with a concrete divider roaming up its middle, and on each side Holiday Inns, discount clothing stores and factory outlets plunked down in disarray. It gets better when you come to Princeton with its farmland and precise rows of trees and, behind, the spires of Holder Hall and the graduate school of Princeton University.

Then Trenton. It is one of those places that people abandon at five o'clock to go elsewhere, if they are lucky, but it is a nice place to work, small and quiet, the pace unhurried. It is dominated, like all state capitals, by one business, the business of state.

Outside Trenton there is beautiful country, farms and small suburban towns with houses that have yards and good schools. Unlike Nevada, New Jersey has seasons. There is a sense of history, of age not found out west. And all of that helped persuade the Gomes family to leave Las Vegas. That and Dennis' eagerness to start a casino investigative effort unburdened by past history and politics, as it had been in Nevada. It never occurred to him that New Jersey would not live up to its promise to let him crusade. It never occurred to him that when he got right down to it, New Jersey would be the same old Nevada story all over again. And then some.

CHAPTER TWENTY-FIVE

Controversy didn't so much explode in New Jersey at the beginning as it did flutter like a full-mast flag anticipating a storm. The first controversy to hit the New Jersey Casino Control Commission was the "Lordi report." In July 1977 Governor Byrne appointed his old friend Essex County prosecutor Joseph Lordi (one of the few pro-casino law enforcement officials) to the post of chairman of the five-person commission. It was to be a full-time job, paying $60,000 a year. Lordi had been first assistant to Byrne when the governor was Essex County prosecutor. Byrne also appointed Lordi's five associate commission members, all of whom would be part-time and on staggered terms and would earn $18,000 a year apiece.

Albert W. Merck of Mendham was appointed to a four-year term. Merck was a former state assemblyman and an heir to the Merck Pharmaceutical fortune. Kenneth M. McDonald of Haddonfield, a car dealer and former mayor of Haddonfield, was appointed for three years. Alice B. Corsey of Deptford, who had been on the Deptford school board, was appointed to a two-year term. (She was the governor's double token: a woman and black.) Prospero DeBona, a Rumson lawyer, was appointed for one year.

It took no longer than its first meeting for the panel to begin bickering. The lines were quickly drawn. The chairman, Joseph Lordi, wanted what some thought were extraordinary powers, and McDonald and DeBona wanted to give them to him. (Corsey was not yet sworn in.) The lone dissenter was Al Merck. He argued, for example, that the hiring of key commission employees warranted a formal policy so that the commission would be free from taint. The others overruled him and immediately voted to let Lordi hire two $38,000-a-year counsels to the commission, Benjamin Cohen and Joseph Fusco, both of whom had been assistant Essex County prosecutors under Lordi.

Merck abstained from the voting and left the meeting early, saying he objected to the procedure being followed. When asked by reporters if Lordi had been given so much authority that it was now a one-man commission, Merck replied, "Ask the commissioner with the power."

The meeting set the tone for the next two and a half years. Lordi would say one thing, and McDonald and Corsey and DeBona—the last two held over after their terms expired—would trot along at his heels in agreement. Merck would remain the only battler. Both Lordi and Merck became heroes—Lordi to the casinos and Merck to the press. Indeed, one of the charges that would most frequently be leveled at the commission was that the setup allowed it to be a one-man show.

Within weeks of the first meeting, Lordi was embroiled in controversy. In June, before Lordi was named to the commission, Governor Byrne had been given a secret state police report that claimed that Lordi had long been associated with organized-crime figures, that he frequented known mob hangouts and that at one time his family law firm represented the brother of a north Jersey mobster, Gerardo "Gerry" Catena. The report noted that as Essex County prosecutor, Lordi had helped get a gun permit for a friend who had a criminal record and who, the police alleged, hobnobbed with crime figures. The former chief of a federal organized-crime task force in New Jersey was quoted as warning his investigators "to stay away from prosecutor Lordi and his office." The state police advised the governor not to appoint Lordi because to do so might cause a stir and lead to major embarrassment to the state's nascent casino industry. The governor ignored the recommendation, appointed Lordi anyway, and sure enough, the state was embarrassed, months later, when the report was leaked.

Lordi was born in the tough Ironbound section of Newark and worked his way up through law school to the lofty heights he had achieved. When he was sworn in to the casino post, he asked a cheering state assembly chamber, "Who would have believed that when I was shooting craps on the sidewalks of Newark, someday I would control gambling?"

Later, in his own defense, he said that the fact that he had "rubbed elbows" with reputed crime figures while young should not disqualify him from the new position. "How long must I go on before I can live down old allegations?" he wondered. Lordi admitted he had eaten and had drinks at places that may have been owned by criminals, but he didn't know it at the time, he said. He also stated that while he knew that Gerardo Catena was a reputed mob figure, he had heard no such allegations about his brother. He said no one could call him soft on crime, that when he was director of the State Alcoholic Beverage Control Division, he created the first unit in the state to control organized crime.

As to that quote from the federal investigation chief about avoiding Lordi and his office, Lordi attributed that to "a vague feeling of corruption in Newark."

Brendan Byrne defended his appointment. The allegations were not new, he said, and they contained no substance. Any questions arising from the police report had been answered to his satisfaction.

The Division of Gaming Enforcement, for its part, managed in the beginning to avoid the controversial limelight in which the commission was cast. Dennis Gomes had arrived and set about hiring investigators for his Special Investigations Bureau. The bureau would handle the heavyweight probes of casinos, their executives and the ancillary companies that served them. Dennis was looking for investigators with strong accounting backgrounds, preferably from varying fields, like the IRS and FBI, accounting firms, even state troopers. He wanted to put together what he called a "hybrid investigator"—a group of people who could take their disparate training, meld it and become as one investigator with the skills of many.

By late 1977, the SIB was around twenty strong and was given its first big assignment: Resorts International. Investigators were enthusiastic about it because it would mean visiting exotic places like Switzerland and the Bahamas, and perhaps more important, it seemed to be an exciting story, if all the newspaper accounts were any indication. In fact, one of the early assignments of some of the investigators was to talk to reporters who had written articles on Resorts. I was contacted by the division about my *Barron's* article, and I also got a call from commission member Al Merck, who took polite exception to my inference that Resorts would probably be licensed because it had spread so much money around the state.

Merck said that was not the way it was going to be. Politics and politicians would have nothing to do with it. The commission alone, uninfluenced, would decide who would get a license and who wouldn't. He said he personally was "underwhelmed" by the $50 million or $60 million being dangled in front of legislators' eyes, and equally underwhelmed by the millions already spent.

It might be noted, as a sidelight, that any reporter writing in what might be perceived as a negative sense could expect lots of reaction from unofficial bodies as well. A lot of it would be friendly, from people who wrote, "Nice story," and signed their names. Those letters were neat and legibly written or typed. But there were other letters, written in chicken scrawl, unsigned or signed by people who turned out not to exist, letters that said, Shut up, lay off, drop dead. And there were sad letters too. I got one from a man from Philadelphia who wanted to know why it was that every time a poor little individual investor bought stock in a company like Resorts International, the press dumped on it. How come he had to lose so much money all the time because he wasn't big and he couldn't get the information the important people could? It just wasn't fair, he wrote.

There were phone calls, too, from men who sounded like their tracheas had been through paper shredders, men with a tendency to talk in "dezes" and "dozes," men saying, Shut up, lay off, drop dead. It was enough to make a reporter paranoid.

Once I got paranoid and refused to answer my door on a Saturday afternoon when the caller wouldn't identify himself. I peered through the viewer, but it wasn't very clear. It was a short man, maybe even a midget—clever of those guys to send a midget—and he started speaking Spanish. Every time I asked, "What do you want?" he started speaking Spanish again and kept ringing. That went on for about ten minutes, until I heard a neighbor in the hall and, figuring the midget wouldn't kill me in front of a neighbor, opened the door. There stood a kid, a fourteen-year-old kid with frightened eyes, clutching a bag of chicken from the local butcher. Paranoia could be a silly business.

CHAPTER TWENTY-SIX

The state's investigation of Resorts International had barely begun by the spring of 1978, but Resorts was already disgusted and impatient and it wasn't shy about making either sentiment felt. It railed against the cost of the probe—it would eventually total a million dollars, not atypical by Nevada standards—and the amount of time it was taking. The company's hotel, renamed the Palace, then later the Resorts International, had been open for months. The casino could be ready with three weeks' notice, and here they were faced with all these delays.

The governor was feeling pressured. Only the preceding winter, he had managed to pull off one of the most dramatic political comebacks in New Jersey history. Incumbent or not, he had been trailing his opponent, Ray Bateman, by miles, according to the polls, and Bateman, incredibly, had made one of the campaign isues the fact that a year after passage of the casino referendum, there was no casino opened. He blamed foot-dragging by Byrne. So even though he had won, the casino issue was no doubt still a sensitive one for Byrne and he was still feeling pressure from many directions.

If Brendan Byrne felt political pressure, then his new attorney general, John Degnan, also felt it, as did Robert Martinez, the head of the Division of Gaming Enforcement. Lobbyist Joel Sterns, too, was undoubtedly getting pressure from his client Resorts International. All in all, Trenton and Atlantic City were in a high-pressure state.

The Resorts International investigation was many months from completion, a fact that in itself drew criticism from some legislators, who had to be reminded that this was not the local supermarket being investigated; it was a complicated financial entity with a long history, a lot of subsidiaries and some strange associations. Add to that the fact that the bulk of its assets were in the Bahamas, a country whose leaders were not receptive to letting outsiders come down and poke around.

Then someone came up with a bright idea. To this day, no one is sure whose idea it was, but politicians and interested onlookers alike stand in line to take the credit. Some say the governor suggested it, some the attorney general. The most widespread opinion has it that it was lawyer Joel Sterns' idea, no doubt at the behest of his client Resorts. One person who didn't want the credit was Dennis Gomes, because he was dead set against it. The plan: to give Resorts International a temporary permit to operate a casino. A six-month permit, renewable for ninety days, if necessary, would be granted. That way, it was argued, everyone would be happy. The investigators would not feel so much pressure to wrap up the investigation, Resorts would not be so cranky, the casino would roll, the governor could breathe easy, the state could begin taxing the new Atlantic City money machine and millions would flow into the state coffers.

Dennis Gomes didn't quite see it that way. Under New Jersey casino law, the American legal premise that a man is innocent until proven guilty is reversed. In the New Jersey casino world, a company has to prove it is worthy of a license, that it is, in effect, innocent. Gomes felt that if you gave a casino a temporary license, you would throw the burden of proof back at the state. Once the casino was open, you would be able to remove it only if you could prove criminality beyond the shadow of a doubt. It was rarely that simple in the casino world. It was tough to find pictures of casino executives handing bags of money to Meyer Lansky (though some executives have made the mistake of being photographed playing golf with Gerardo Catena). Associations and inference play a large part. Gomes felt—and his team agreed—that once you let Resorts International into Atlantic City on a temporary basis, you would never get them out.

Gomes and his staff had been to Paradise Island. They had conducted a surprise raid on the casino, sealed the filing cabinets in the executive offices, in the process upsetting not only the company's executives but Bahamian officials too. Bahamian laws were being broken, it was said, by all those unauthorized persons entering restricted areas of the casino— as if it were the first time that had happened. Davis insisted on watching the investigators as they took page after page out of the files, and he hastily summoned other executives from up north.

Soon after the investigators got back to New Jersey, Dennis Gomes developed a hypothesis, which, true to his usual method of operation, he would "test" with all information gleaned after that point. His hypothesis started with the 1960 visit by Meyer Lansky to Stafford Sands: Sands had stated that Lansky offered him $2 million to let him run casinos in the Bahamas, and that he turned Lansky down. Gomes hypothesized that that wasn't so. Perhaps Sands told Lansky he was too obvious and would have to find suitable front men. Lansky came up with Groves-Chesler, runs the Gomes hypothesis, and later with Mary Carter Paint Company. Dennis Gomes thought Resorts had been told by Lansky, You can have the restaurants, the hotels, the golf course, anything else you want, but keep your hands off our casino. Gomes thought Resorts was linked to the mob and that he could prove it.

But he had a ways to go. There were many avenues yet to explore. For example, the investigators had been searching for a woman named Donna Wilson, a long-time girlfriend of James Crosby who was alleged to be a "baglady" for Resorts, carrying illicit goods between the Bahamas and Miami and to such far-flung areas as Alaska. The investigators looked for her quietly because they feared that if Resorts knew they were looking, they might get to her first.

In recommending against a temporary license until he could prove his theory, Dennis was bucking a powerful political establishment. Gomes was all but alone. The most vocal group in agreement with him was the Citizens Casino Surveillance Coalition, comprised of clergymen and citizens who devoted spare time to it. Its secretary, the Reverend Howard Abbott, said, "Already we see an attempt to short-circuit a long and involved process of investigation . . . that even questionable firms might obtain access to casino permits." The group was ineffective and ignored, except by Resorts International, which threatened to sue.

Governor Byrne pushed through the legislature a bill amending casino legislation to allow temporary permits. It was quickly approved, in March of 1978. If Resorts still did not have a license after the nine months allowed in the legislation, the casino would be run by trustees whom Resorts International would be allowed to pick. The arrangement brought howls of disapproval from Nevada, which pointed out that New Jersey had lost little time in allowing the erosion of the world's so-called strictest casino laws.

After the formalities were dispensed with, there were weeks of commission hearings. Resorts was targeting May—perhaps Memorial Day weekend—as its opening date, but there were matters that remained to be discussed: How many tables would there be, and what kinds? How large a staff was needed? Was Resorts ready for the maximum numbers of everything from people to cars? The toughest questioner, as usual, was commission member Al Merck. Resorts brought in a consultant to say that the staff was plentiful, trained and willing. He gave facts and figures to support that contention but, under Merck's probing, admitted that he had gotten the numbers from a Resorts vice-president, Steve Norton.

State regulations fell like dominoes as Resorts was granted concession after concession so that it might open quickly. In sessions frequently marked by heated disagreements between Lordi and Merck, the commission waived a rule that no casino could buy more than half of its slot machines from any one source. That wasn't convenient for Resorts, which would buy all of them from Bally. The commission also waived licensing requirements on hundreds of ancillary companies servicing the hotel and casino. And it licensed individuals, like casino pit bosses, even though they had not filed the required financial statements. And for the time being, Resorts would not be made to put percentage payout meters on its slot machines. The company promised that its payout would be 85 percent, higher than the state's required 83 percent, but later on it developed that it hadn't even lived up to the state requirement.

The most heated of all issues was that involving minimums and maximums of play. A minimum is the least a gambler can put up to play a certain game. The maximum is the most he is allowed to bet. Minimums and maximums are not an issue in Nevada because in Las Vegas there is competition among casinos. If a gambler thinks minimums are too high, he can go to another casino where they are lower. In the New Jersey discussions, the lines were quickly drawn. Resorts wanted minimums high, Al Merck wanted them low. Resorts argued that with low minimums, high-stake gamblers would be forced to mix at the tables with inexperienced types who had a tendency to get their hands in the way of the dice. Resorts also contended that with low minimums, people who shouldn't be gambling would lose money. James Crosby said, "We are not in the business of cashing social security checks."

Merck countered that with *high* minimums, people who shouldn't be gambling would lose even more money. Merck knew that a casino manager's dream is the guy who sits down at the table, loses his whole bankroll in three turns and vacates his seat to make room for the next loser. And Merck knew that high maximums scared the house because they feared that a gambler who felt that his lucky roll was going to be the next one would put too much money on the line. Merck further argued that with high minimums, patrons would be driven to cheaper "sucker" games with rotten odds, like the big six wheel or the slots.

The argument dragged well into May, still unsettled only days before the casino was scheduled to open. That fact terrified Merck, who foresaw a colossal customer rip-off by the casino.

At a late May meeting, a proposal was set forth by a commission staffer calling for half the tables to carry one- and two-dollar minimums. Lawyer Joel Sterns was a perfect study in effrontery. He rose from his seat and announced that he was "shocked" by the proposal. Jack Davis said, "If my voice sounds rather dry, it's because I'm even more shocked." Then they went through their favorite argument: if the commission forced them to have such low minimums, no one else was going to be interested in investing in Atlantic City. In fact, Davis said, if they had known the commission would insist on these kinds of rules, they would probably never have made a $50 million investment themselves. (It was an oft-heard argument. For example, many months earlier, when the rate at which the state would tax the casinos was being discussed,

Resorts threatened that a proposed rate was too high and would keep investors out. It was lowered.)

Merck argued that bettors were consumers and their rights should be protected. Lordi's stand was that "I am more concerned with attracting investors to Atlantic City than in attracting bettors."

James Crosby, the Resorts chairman, stage-whispered the verbal equivalent of the shot heard round the world. He leaned toward lawyer Sterns and said, "I have serious reservations about opening with dollar minimums."

Not open? Just days before the scheduled event? How could they do that? The governor had promised, the mayor had promised, the people were waiting. The governor was to officiate at a pre-opening party. It was unthinkable not to open. It was so unthinkable that a compromise was reached and four commissioners approved it. Merck did not. By opening day, there was not a dollar-minimum sign in view. Ninety percent of the tables required an ante of five dollars or more. The state had knuckled under.

CHAPTER TWENTY-SEVEN

Memorial Day weekend, May 26, 1978. The crowd began to gather hours before the scheduled ten o'clock opening; the lines snaked up the Boardwalk. People had come from near and far, but mostly near—Ridley Township, Pennsylvania, Ocean City, New Jersey, Philadelphia. They wore everything from suits and ties to Bermuda shorts to Hawaiian shirts, but they had a common purpose: to be part of history, partake of one of the sure-to-be-most-memorable events in the history of the Garden State, the opening of the first East Coast casino, the first legal American casino outside Nevada.

When the doors opened, the scene was wild. People raced for the tables, pushing and maneuvering, desperate for a chance to leave their mark in the form of five or fifty or a thousand dollars left at the tables. The tables were jammed ten and twenty deep. You couldn't move through the aisles. The smoke was so thick, it was as if the place was on fire. The dealers were bewildered virgins, innocents to the ways of gamblers. Gamblers were unseasoned, too, many of them, and play was slow as rules were explained.

The commission inspectors and the enforcers from Gaming might almost as well have not been there for all the good they could do in a crowd like that. They couldn't tell who was taking money on what tray to what booth, which chips were being transported where, who was entering or leaving the cage or whether or not the woman manning the slot-change booth had a license. Better to rush out to the beach and tell the ocean to hold back.

And still people waited on the Boardwalk, for three and four and five hours. So scarce was gambling space in those early days, one possibly apocryphal story has it, that bettors unwilling to vacate their space for a trip to the men's room simply relieved themselves under the tables. Perhaps they were better off. Some people who ventured into the men's room were accosted by "bathroom bandits" and relieved of their winnings. Governor Byrne had promised tasteful European-style gambling in Atlantic City. So far, he had promised wrong.

Still, the opening was to cause vibrations up and down the coast and across the sea and, not least, would send shock waves across the floors of the nation's financial centers. This was the closest thing America had seen in a century to a gold rush. Everyone wanted in on it.

You could almost picture the scene later in corporate board rooms across America. A casino company in Atlantic City was packing them in and turning them away, and it was making close to a million dollars a day doing it. Several companies had already made plans to set up shop on the Boardwalk, but others had waited to see how Resorts fared. Now they plunged forward. Some had never considered it at all until that week, when they saw what harvests could be reaped, not only in Atlantic City but in the stock market.

Reese Palley had said, "It's a no-brains business." Plenty of brainless people were jumping into the fray. Overnight, scads of companies from tombstone makers to computer concerns to meat packers swept up options on land and announced that they had bought a piece of the action. Sometimes they announced it before the deal went through. It didn't matter to them and it didn't matter to stock buyers. They might as well have been shooting craps on the floor of the New York and American stock exchanges for all fundamental analysis had to do with it.

There were people who had been on Wall Street for fifty years, who had seen bulls and bears and booms and busts, crashes and roaring rallies, and even they couldn't believe it. In the summer of 1978, the activity inside one Atlantic City casino spilled over in delirious abandon to the nation's securities markets, and in a period of months, casino stocks tacked on a gigantic billion dollars' worth of market value. People wanted casino stocks, badly. *The Wall Street Journal* reported that a man chained himself to a Merrill Lynch office door, refusing to leave until he was allowed to buy more casino stocks. One financial man told a customer in disgust that he was a stockbroker, not a croupier, but other brokers knew a sure thing when they saw it. All they had to do was mention the word "casino" and they had a sale.

The same went for those companies, those meat packers and tombstone manufacturers. Stocks that hadn't moved above three dollars in five years were suddenly doubling and tripling in a week. Never mind that some of the companies were courting bankruptcy. Never mind that in some cases the land they had optioned had already been optioned by someone else, or wasn't zoned for casinos, or wasn't big enough for a chicken coop. Forget the fact that they had never operated a casino before, or that even if they lay down on the floor of Chase chairman David Rockefeller's office and held their breath, they *still* wouldn't get financing. And never mind that even if they could get land *and* a license *and* money, it would be years before they could open. Nobody seemed to care.

A lot of the buyers were small investors, individuals who plundered savings accounts or sold their other stocks or margined themselves to the hilt for the same reason that a lot of people bet the horses—it would make them rich, they'd be on easy street, their troubles would be over. And these weren't $2 stocks they were buying: Resorts International was selling at $150, Caesar's World of New Jersey at $50, Bally at $50. Yet the people clamored for more and a lot of them got hurt. Some of the investors got caught up in the delirium and the greed, followed the stocks upward, then crashed back down to earth with them, much poorer.

The Resorts International stockholder meeting of 1978 was like a pep rally and revival meeting rolled into one. Everyone who was there had made money. The stock was still way up. The hosannas rang from the rafters in the Resorts International Hotel. Stockholders stood in the aisles and shouted the praises of Crosby and Davis—what wonderful managers they were, what excellent executives, they had made everyone rich. No one mentioned how upset some had been when, months before the referendum, Resorts officers had voted themselves options to buy Resorts stock at $4. In the period June through September 1978, president Jack Davis, for one, unloaded 27,000 shares of stock on the market and took in more than $3 million. It was okay because everyone else was getting rich too.

The scene a year later, in the same place, had a different mood. In the intervening months, the stock had climbed even higher and had split three for one, to hover in the area of $60. Then the shooting star fell earthward with the same velocity with which it had shot up. At the annual meeting of 1979, people who had bought low were still happy, but people who had paid too much and worried about recouping their losses plaintively asked management, "Couldn't you please, for those of us who paid so much, institute a dividend?" Resorts International, plumper by $200 million in revenues, said no.

There was nothing shareholders could do about it. Resorts

International said the kind of people who bought its stock were more interested in capital appreciation than dividends. And Resorts International had proven, by its close-knit board of directors, that it wasn't interested in outside interference. Thousands of individual investors banding together would be virtually powerless to do anything about it because their A shares each had only one hundreth the voting power of the B shares.

Small investors were not the only ones who got caught up in the gambling craze. Wall Street security analysts did too. Before Atlantic City, it was a rare analyst who paid attention to gambling at all. No public company had ever made a killing in Las Vegas because by the time they got there, there was too much competition. You would have thought Wall Street would quickly understand the application of that fact to Atlantic City, that Resorts International was making a fortune because it had the only game in town. If they did understand, they weren't taking much note of it.

When the Atlantic City fever started, brokerage houses rushed to find someone to follow the gambling stocks, often putting their "leisure-time" analysts on the job. Few of them got there when the stocks were selling at two or four or even forty. Virtually every analyst missed the huge early leg of the rise, but that didn't stop them from churning out a paper blitz of hundreds of thousands of sheets' worth of memos. Analysts who had never set foot in a casino were overnight experts on the drop and the take and the minimums and the maximums. They spewed forth analyses of how much Atlantic City would make and who would get what share of the pie. They subscribed to Walt Tyminski's *Rouge et Noir,* then begged to differ with his evaluations. They listened to commission member Al Merck's crusades and sneered that he was naïve. Often they were dead wrong and rarely did they use common sense. A Merrill Lynch analyst noted in an early 1980 report that estimates of construction costs on the first phase of Bally's casino were off—by more than $200 million! Several other analysts kept hammering out recommendations—especially of Resorts International—as the stock went further and further down.

There was not an analyst on the Street, incidentally, who stopped to look at the moral issues. They didn't care who had cheated whom, who was mob and who wasn't, who had dealt with whom, as long as they were going to make money. It might be added, too, that the Securities and Exchange Commission, guardian of investors, waited until September 1978, the top of the market, to warn potential buyers that gambling stocks might be dangerous.

Institutional Investor, a magazine that caters to the financial community, ran a cover story on Paine Webber analyst Lee Isgur, who followed casinos (and had followed a few before Atlantic City). They described some months in his life:

In October, it was a probing investigation of the glittering entertainment facilities of the MGM Grand Hotel and Caesar's Palace in Las Vegas. Then followed a day bowling on the lanes of several local alleys. Immediately thereafter came a flight to Hawaii for an in-depth analysis of the Hilton Hawaiian Village in Honolulu. In November, as the unremitting grind continued, it was off to Reno with dinner and a ringside seat for the MGM Hotel's spectacular stage revue, *Hello Hollywood.* After two days there and being exposed to the danger of chlorine poisoning from the swimming pool in the afternoon and the fatigue of round-the-clock gaming rooms in the night, it was a wearying ride to Lake Tahoe—just in time for the midnight show at Harrah's . . .

And on it went.

Isgur replied, "Actually those were killing trips." He told *Institutional Investor:*

The days start early and the nights can be long. You have to go to all of the receptions and buffets because that's when you meet the corporate officials informally and get to know the quality of company management. You have to go to the shows to see what kind of entertainment the public is getting. Observing the gambling, of course, is essential to understanding the casino's operation. I am constantly working. When I was at the Hawaiian Village and they told me the best room I could get was one of the $54 *el cheapos,* my ears really started ringing because that meant they were having no trouble filling up in spite of extremely high room rates.

Security analysts fall into many of the same traps that "beat" reporters do. They are afraid that if they are too harsh on a company, management will cut them dead. Managements are adept at playing the game. A company chief knows that if he lets an analyst call him by his first name, if he lunches the analyst at Lutèce and drops him off afterward in his limousine, and if he tells him, "Listen, I really shouldn't be telling you this because I haven't told anyone else, but . . ."—then he has won half the battle.

Thus, when Resorts was in danger of losing its license in New Jersey, a plausible rumor had it that the company was negotiating to sell its assets to another company just in case. But one analyst told me that he had called Jim Crosby and Jim said it wasn't true and he believed it because Jim had told him personally.

But as some analysts will admit, security analysis is an imprecise art. In the case of gambling stocks, many of them happened eventually to be right or lucky, depending on how you looked at it. When Resorts was selling at fifty dollars, some people thought it was too high and some thought it too low. The ones who thought it was too high said sure, it had a temporary monopoly, but earnings would quickly slide when competition came to town. They were right on the long-term fundamentals, but wrong on the stock price. The people who took the opposite tack were wrong on the fundamentals, but right on the stock price. So who was lucky and who was smart?

The fact is, some of the so-called smartest money on Wall Street got burned in the stock of Resorts International, and not necessarily because they bought too high. A lot of "short-sellers" got into trouble too, one of whom was Bob Wilson. Robert Wilson was one of those spectacular Wall Street success stories. When he was thirty, he quit a job in a bank trust department, took $15,000 his father gave him and proceeded to parlay it into tens of millions. From 1965 to 1977, Wilson's portfolio grew at a compound annual rate of 35 percent. In 1978 he took a colossal financial bath, and all because of one stock, Resorts International.

Wilson's specialty was short-selling. Most people buy stock "long," meaning that they think its future prospects are good and they expect the stock to rise in price. Short-sellers work with stocks they think are going to go down. When they think the price of a stock is overinflated, they borrow some of its shares from a broker, promising to return them later. When the stock price declines, they buy shares at the market price to "cover" their short or return what they have borrowed. The money they make is the spread between the price they borrowed (and sold) it at and that at which they replaced it. Short-selling is a very risky business. If the stock goes up instead of down, the short-seller gets squeezed. He is forced to replace the stock by buying it at much higher prices than he borrowed it at. It took tangling with Resorts International to get Bob Wilson to say, "Now I know why everybody is afraid to short stocks."

Resorts International, like most companies, is not fond of short-sellers. And Resorts may be less sanguine than most because there are more shorts hanging around its stock. Over the years Resorts has aroused more than a degree of skepticism in many a financial soul. A company like IBM doesn't have to worry about it so much. IBM is regarded as an investment vehicle, not an on-again, off-again speculation like Resorts.

To explain the high short interest in its shares, Resorts began routinely to accuse various people of saying or writing negative things because they were consorting with the short-sellers. They said that these people were trying to make the price of the stock go down so that they might reap financial rewards. For example, they claimed that *Barron's* writers were tipping off shorts that they were going to write a negative story; the shorts would then take a bigger short position, *Barron's* would publish a negative story and the price of the stock would go down. Then, went their story, *Barron's* would get a cut of the money the short had made. It was untrue.

Barron's was only one of their targets. They also made the claims about *Rouge et Noir* editor Walt Tyminski when he turned negative on them, and they said it about the little New Jersey Citizens Casino Surveillance Coalition, many of whose members didn't even know what a short sale was. They no doubt wove Bob Wilson into their conspiracy theory too.

In a talk with *Barron's* editors in late 1977, Bob Wilson disclosed that he was short Resorts International because he thought the public was dead wrong in its assessment of the company and Atlantic City. He didn't think Atlantic City was going to do that well, and he thought that Resorts International, in particular, would have problems because it would be its first experience with competition and with operators who were a lot more skilled than it was. The mistake he made—and a lot of intelligent people made it—was failing to realize that the state of New Jersey would give Resorts a one-year head start on the competition.

Wilson began shorting the stock at around $80. When it rose, he wasn't worried—he simply shorted more. By the spring of 1978, he was short more than 200,000 shares, at prices ranging from $8 to $25. Leaving the position where it was, he embarked on a long-planned six-month tour of Europe and the Far East. He could not have picked a worse time. Shortly after he left, the Resorts International Atlantic City casino opened, was a huge success, and investors started diving into the stock. Bob Wilson was soon losing hundreds of thousands of dollars a day.

The stock kept rising as Wilson prowled the markets of India and dined in the great restaurants of Europe. He was receiving panicky letters and phone calls from his brokers in New York. They didn't know what to do. Wilson, the infallible market-gazer, the omnipotent short-seller, was getting wiped out. Wilson told them to stand firm. A good short-seller had to have nerves of steel. Wilson had always been good. He knew the Resorts balloon had to burst. There was no reason why the stock should be so high. It would tumble at any moment.

Wilson's plight was worsened by stockbrokers who used his short position to talk clients into buying Resorts International stock. It has to go up, they would say, because Bob Wilson is short over 200,000 shares. When he is forced to cover, he will only drive the price higher because he will be buying so much stock. (Bob Wilson wasn't alone in his short position. There was a mountain of short interest in the stock.)

Wilson's brokers kept interrupting his wanderings with their constant calls. They told him they would have to liquidate some of his other holdings to satisfy margin requirements. They said they were putting a limit on how far the stock could run up before they covered the shorts. They didn't want to take the risk that if Bob Wilson suffered a financial collapse he would take them with him.

Wilson covered some of his shares and his covering forced the stock price higher. By the time the price reached into the hundreds, he had lost $10 million. The broker cables were increasingly frantic. The stock was at $150, $160, $170. It marched on. The nerves of steel began to shatter. He knew the end had to be near, knew the stock could go no further, but he couldn't take the chance.

In early September, from Taipei, he Telexed his brokers. The message was succinct: COVER ALL RESORTS. Then he went sightseeing. The next day he toured some more, and when he returned to his hotel room in the evening, there was a call from his brokers. Resorts was at $190. What should they do? They hadn't gotten the Telex. He repeated the unreceived instructions. When the deed was done, Bob Wilson had lost somewhere in the neighborhood of $20 million.

CHAPTER TWENTY-EIGHT

On a Tuesday night in November of 1978, at what was still Atlantic City's only casino, the aisles were choked with people and the air was choked with smoke, filled with the din and the clamor of coins hitting metal, chips bouncing on felt, gamblers exhorting their dice. It was not the European-style gambling New Jersey was supposed to have. It was more akin to a downtown Vegas grind joint. Buttock-baring cocktail waitresses dispensed drinks to the tables. A man shouted across to a buddy that he just got laid and it was so good he cried like a girl. Music blasted out from the nearby cocktail lounges; its volume had increased through the evening for the same reason that the air-conditioning had been turned to bone-chilling levels. Casinos think it makes people gamble.

Seven tourists from Ridley Township, Pennsylvania, occupied seven seats at a blackjack table. They had been there since ten in the morning; it was now midnight. They had not been lucky for the most part, losing all morning and into the afternoon. Suddenly, though, in the evening their luck had changed. They were ahead fifteen hundred dollars. It must be a streak: they were gliding toward euphoria. But abruptly, a pit boss approached and without a word removed the table's five-dollar-minimum sign, slamming in its place a twenty-five-dollar sign. Strictly illegal.

A woman protested. "We've played at this table three times a week since the casino opened and it's always been a five-dollar table. You can't change it now."

"Try and stop me, lady."

"You're an idiot," she told him.

"You're the idiot, lady."

The other players began to protest. They wouldn't move, they said, and they would have to be dragged screaming from the casino. One woman shouted so other tables could hear, "We've been at this table since ten o'clock this morning and now they want to change the minimum because we're winning."

"I'm a shareholder in this company," declared a man, "and we're not going to take this kind of treatment. I'm gonna see Jack Davis tomorrow."

"Calm down," his wife told him. "Your heart. My husband is a heart patient," she explained to the gathering crowd.

The argument continued perhaps ten minutes more, with insults traded between customers and dealer and pit boss. Finally, the pit boss told the gamblers he would allow one more "shoe" of cards to be dealt before the minimum changed. The gamblers were having none of it. They refused to move and they refused to pay up. The pit boss gave in. With an oily smirk, he announced he had good news: the stake would remain five dollars.

When the incident was related to a Casino Control Commission inspector, he commented, "Oh, that's a common occurrence. We can't really do anything unless the customer files a formal complaint, and even then we can't do much."

The law: before a minimum is changed, the patrons must be

given notice and allowed to play the shoe in progress and at least two more full shoes, a process estimated to take roughly a half-hour.

It had been six months since Resorts International had blazed the East Coast casino trail and thrown its doors hastily open. But what a half year it had been. Already the op art-colored rug was scarred by a million cigarette butts ground in by a million feet. Already a million and a half gamblers had dropped better than $100 million at the tables and wheels and slots. Already Resorts had thrown one of its famous publicity weekends, though this time it wasn't so successful because few of the stars came out for it.

Still, for Resorts International these were very profitable times. They had pulled off one of the biggest business coups ever. And these were, no doubt, satisfying times in other ways. The former paint company had been reborn years earlier as a casino concern, but always its corporate identity was shrouded behind names like Paradise Island Casino and Britannia Beach Hotel. Now it had come of age, had emerged a superstar in Atlantic City, and the name Resorts International was emblazoned everywhere, on every available piece of green felt, every towel, every ashtray and, most spectacularly, high in the sky, brilliantly lit on the hotel tower.

But controversy had clung to Resorts through all the years, and the first six months in Atlantic City were no exception. In the early weeks of the casino, a tray with $14,000 worth of chips disappeared. Some $180,000 was embezzled or lost or misplaced from the slot machines and, the Division of Gaming Enforcement claimed, Resorts knew but failed to report it.

Throughout the months, too, Al Merck of the casino commission continued to fight. His reputation as the maverick commissioner was spreading; he was, it was thought, the one most likely to stand between Resorts International and a permanent license. He made it his business to learn gambling, visiting Las Vegas, taking courses, becoming versed in the subtleties of the games. When he was in Atlantic City for commission meetings, he made it a practice to tour the casino late at night, unannounced and unheralded, to see if it was being run according to Hoyle. He was often unhappy with what he found.

Merck was peeved by Resorts' constant inattention to the rules. The commissioner would wander from table to table, peer over the tops of the players' heads to see the minimum signs. He was not unobtrusive as he scribbled notes in a pad or on the backs of envelopes, a slouched, skinny linguini of a man in an oversized suit and tie, a conservative outfit almost an oddity in the Resorts casino. Sometimes he noticed that the two-dollar and five-dollar tables were not the required percentage of the total, even though at some more expensive tables dealers dealt idly to themselves or to only one player while players waited for space at the cheap ones.

Merck was also unhappy that slot-booth-change windows didn't advertise the availability of loose change, that you could get two dollars' worth of quarters, not just ten- and twenty-dollar rolls, as most gamblers thought. Merck was afraid that customers would be intimidated into buying—and losing—more than they could afford. He had pushed, too, for the availability of rule books, not just the glossy promos the house offered, but ones that gave odds for the various games and other information that might help a player bet more intelligently. He had won that fight, but usually when he visited, he found the casino was out of the books. One night in November, a casino official told him with a sneer that they just couldn't keep them in stock.

On November 9, 1978, the day following one of Merck's nocturnal tours, the five casino commissioners sat in a dreary hearing room stuck away in a corner of the convention center in Atlantic City. Lordi lit and relit his pipe; Merck appeared to sleep; Corsey looked fresh and immaculate, omnipresent flower in her buttonhole; DeBona, with his small body and prominent nose, looked like a bird perched for flight; and last there was McDonald, his head drooping into his hands. They listened as Resorts brought forth witnesses to support the familiar fight it was fighting that day: the one for higher minimums.

They produced Peter Aranow, an investment banker from the New York firm of Bear Stearns, Resorts' underwriter. He testified that low minimums would surely cripple the ability of Atlantic City to obtain financing. He said investors didn't want to commit money to industries that were subject to the whims of overzealous bureaucrats. Look at the trouble Las Vegas had raising money in the beginning, he said. And now there were companies in Atlantic City having trouble getting financing. He warned of "boom and bust" scenarios. When investors get scared, they rush for the exits, and good companies can get hurt too. Investors may want to put money somewhere else where the return is not as great but neither is the risk.

Aranow failed to point out that even as he was speaking, the stock market was making its own assessment. Investors *were* rushing for the exits and bailing out of the gambling stocks, but for reasons quite apart from minimums and maximums. He also failed to note that in the early days, Las Vegas was just steps ahead of old Western shoot-'em-up towns, run by a pack of mobsters. And he didn't say that gambling had always been and would always be hands-off for large numbers of institutional lenders who didn't want to risk the taint, no matter what the minimums.

Also testifying was Frank Fee, a commission auditor. He said he had conducted a study, finding that the two- and five-dollar tables were always full at the Resorts casino and there were always bettors waiting for a space. By contrast, large numbers of seats stood empty at the more expensive tables. The public was voting unmistakably in favor of low minimums.

Nor was controversy confined to the commission hearing room. On that same day in November in the early morning hours, after months of legal tangles over its disposition, after it had been declared a historic landmark, the Marlborough-Blenheim Hotel, rotunda and all, was blown out of existence. It had been one of the most distinguishing marks on the face of Atlantic City, but its destruction was in keeping with what the governor said he wanted for Atlantic City. After Resorts had hastily reopened in a renovated building, the governor decided he wanted new buildings, new construction, no "patch-and-paint" jobs. His wish was granted as one hotel after another was felled by the blasts of the demolition crews. (And as his wish was granted, Resorts' monopoly was prolonged.) In the place of the hotels, builders began to erect modern, often phantasmic glass-and-steel monoliths. The skyline eventually would resemble nothing so much as one of those false fronts in a Hollywood back lot, and behind it the same old Atlantic City.

Shops and slums were two other matters for acrimony. Many of the shopkeepers along the Boardwalk, who had looked toward casinos as the key to their personal prosperity, were being thown out by landlords trying to woo Gucci or Cartier or someone equally glamorous and capable of paying higher rents.

The slums were not so easily dismissed. A master planner hired to plot Atlantic City's future proposed that the South Inlet section, home to thousands of low-income Hispanics, be razed. The outcry that greeted the proposal led him to amend his plan. The slums should not be razed until somebody figured out what to do with all those people.

But that began to take care of itself, without much state or municipal interference. Between the referendum of late 1976 and mid-1979, according to a survey, about 70 percent of the lots in the South Inlet changed hands. Latin organizations estimated that in the same period, the Hispanic population plunged from 7,500 to around 2,000. The city thought those figures were too high. One Hispanic leader said, "This city has to wake up and realize the human suffering involved." Mayors along the Jersey coast complained that they had enough problems of their own without having to deal with indigent former Atlantic City residents who were wandering in their direction.

The Hispanics were forced out in a number of ways: Homes were burned down. City inspectors suddenly took an interest in long-unenforced housing codes so that landlords could evict the tenants. Rents were pumped up. Landlords began to blame tenants for existing building violations and demanded that they vacate. Landlords refused to provide tenants with written leases.

Blacks were no less furious than Hispanics. From the opening days of the casino, they were picketing with signs that read, WE WERE USED. Blacks had been coaxed to vote for the referendum—and were generally credited as being the swing factor—by promises that they would get better jobs. They claimed that they were getting only the menial ones and that what they earned didn't even pay for the higher rents they were being forced to come up with.

It didn't take long, either, before senior citizens were crying rip-off. They said that the way the system was set up, they would be only pennies better off per person than they had been before. Within a year, the bureaucratic structure set up to dispense the casino revenue funds to the elderly was collapsing under its own weight. State officials were forced to admit that they had dramatically underestimated the cost of the program for the elderly, which, incidentally, had been a Byrne campaign pledge.

In Atlantic City it was getting so that people were afraid to look at the mail because it might carry a notice that the new owner was raising the rent by a factor of two or three or four, to levels that could not be covered by a whole month's social security.

There was one story, revolving around houses on a beachfront block, that could have been written for *The Twilight Zone. Penthouse*, the girlie "men's" magazine organization, wanted to build on the block, but first they had to clear it of dozens of small houses. They offered each homeowner $100,000 to sell, but only if all agreed to sell. One by one they sold, but in the end there were three pesky holdouts—Vera Coking, owner of the Sea Shell Boardinghouse, Mrs. Anthony Bongiovanni and Morris and Esther Miller. Some people called them greedy, said they were holding out for more money, but they said that wasn't the way it was at all. They had lived on that street for decades and they planned to die there. Some of their neighbors began to harass them.

Penthouse raised the ante to $200,000 each, then $275,000, perhaps even higher. Rumors abounded. A construction worker said he'd heard that one house was offered $1 million, but that was highly doubtful. Whatever the figure, these three households wouldn't budge. Even so, *Penthouse* was not about to cede its Boardwalk frontage, so it gave all the other homeowners their money, razed the rest of the block and proceeded to take some inconvenient twists and turns in its steelwork to route the building around the houses.

It ended up being a sad solution. Mrs. Bongiovanni, a woman in her sixties whose husband had died while the debate was going on, tried to live her life as usual, but one of her favorite pastimes, gardening, was lost to her. Digging and planting had become a dangerous activity with the risk of steel splinters and debris falling from above. Besides that, there wasn't any sun anymore. The steelwork had blotted it out. Ms. Coking, it turned out, probably would have to give up her Sea

Shell Boardinghouse anyway. The city raised the assessed value of the house from just over $20,000 to over $100,000. She would never be able to pay the taxes.

As time went on, other effects of casinos became apparent. Swarms of state officials were leaving their posts and showing up on the payrolls at casinos. (The law made it illegal for Division of Gaming Enforcement personnel to do this, but the legislators who wrote that law did not see fit to extend the prohibition to themselves or to the Casino Control Commission.) For example, William Downey, former director of the Atlantic City Housing and Urban Development Agency, became executive director for the Casino Hotel Association lobby. John R. Best, the mayor of Ventnor City, became an investor in and resident partner of Ritz Associates (the company U.S. Senator Harrison Williams allegedly used his influence for). David M. Satz, former U.S. attorney for New Jersey, went on to represent the Casino Hotel Association. Arthur J. Sills, attorney general in the Hughes administration, went on to become counsel to Bally Corporation. And, as noted, Richard Hughes, former governor *and* former State Supreme Court chief justice, joined the law firm that represented Resorts International. Casino Control commissioners stayed at the Resorts hotel at discounts of up to 50 percent, which roused editorial wrath when the press picked up on it.

There were plenty of conflicts of interest too. Assemblyman Kenneth Gewertz was brought before the Joint Legislative Ethics Committee on conflict charges because he owned stock in Bally Corporation, which supplies slot machines to Resorts International and eventually would have its own casino. Gewertz was ruled in conflict. He retaliated by bringing charges against Steven Perskie, the nephew of the Resorts lawyer. The lawyer had died by then, and Steven had become executor of his estate and trustee of several thousand shares of Resorts

International stock. Perskie was also beneficiary to land that was in a casino zone of Atlantic City. By some unfathomable logic, Perskie was cleared of conflict charges. It may have had to do with popularity. Gewertz was not one of the better-liked legislators. He was voted out of office in late 1979 and, shortly after leaving, became enmeshed in what some thought a very funny story of modern-day Atlantic City. He picked up three prostitutes in his Lincoln Continental in Atlantic City and they "rolled" him, robbing him of his watch and other valuables. Gewertz, rather than keep his mouth shut and avoid embarrassing publicity, insisted on seeing the women come to justice. Two of the prostitutes were found and admitted the crime. But they told police they got in the car, quickly summed up Gewertz as a jerk and decided they would be doing a public service if they rolled him.

CHAPTER TWENTY-NINE

In the first seven months of 1978, the crime rate in Atlantic City rose 25 percent, with the greatest part of the bulge coming in the months following the opening of the casino. Prostitution flourished: after dark you could see scores of girls standing around up and down Pacific Avenue. Murder and assault were on the rise, as were larceny and car theft. The city needed more cops, but peculiarities in the laws prevented it from getting them into the budget at first.

Needless to say, organized crime was not keeping to the sidelines. A Canadian Broadcasting Corporation exposé in March 1979 and a lawsuit brought by two Canadian lawyers tied Canadian organized-crime figure Paul Volpe and others to the purchase of more than sixty properties—millions of dollars worth—in Atlantic City. Many organized-crime figures tried—and apparently succeeded in—becoming involved in ancillary businesses serving the casinos. Even before casinos began, State Commission of Investigation hearings revealed that the mob was making major inroads. One witness at the hearings, Angelo Bruno, alleged boss of a Philadelphia "crime family," said he had no interest in the casino business, but it came out that he got two to three cents on every carton of cigarettes sold in Atlantic City. Angelo Bruno was gunned down in his car in front of his Philadelphia home in March 1980.

Law enforcement officials suspect he was one more fatality in an emerging organized-crime war over who would control what in Atlantic City. (Bruno was thought to have ordered the execution of Carmine Galante.) None of this could have come as much of a surprise to New Jersey officials. Only weeks before the Bruno murder, New Jersey Attorney General John Degnan admitted that organized crime had already managed to infiltrate ancillary casino businesses in a big way. He said the state was faced with large law enforcement challenges. But he added that as far as he knew, the mob had not yet infiltrated the casinos themselves.

The costs in law enforcement were not only tangible ones. To ward off continued gains by the mob, top law enforcement investigators were consigned to the business of investigating Atlantic City, leaving the rest of the state under the eyes of less skillful or newer investigators whom it would take years to train. The attorney general, in fact, says that most of his energies are devoted to casino-related undertakings. As for the monetary costs, there was no provision in the casino laws that required casinos to bear the increased cost of law enforcement in Atlantic City and the state, even though the casinos were responsible for the mob's new interest.

The state can expect organized-crime infiltration to have many effects, and they might as well resign themselves to a nonstop battle because that's what they have on their hands. They will never drive organized crime out of Atlantic City. Prostitution, often mob-controlled, will flourish. So will unscrupulous loan sharks, who will prey on bankrupted gamblers, charging them 100 percent or 500 percent or 5,000 percent interest. (There is a body of thought, it might be mentioned, that sees a direct relationship between the amount of money gamblers lose gambling and the rise in the welfare roles.) Some law enforcement officials believe loan sharking is organized crime's most profitable business.

And, too, the mob can be expected to worm its way into some of the casinos and begin to execute skims. As former New Jersey Attorney General William Hyland once put it to a meeting of state legislators: "I can tell you, gentlemen, that for every twenty-four hours you spend thinking about the problems of the state and how to combat organized crime, [organized crime is] spending a month figuring how to get around it. They are very resourceful and very clever."

Nor is theft on a grand scale the only issue. *The New York Times* reported that Atlantic City churches are experiencing a large drop-off in worshipers, partly due to the dwindling populations in once-residential areas, partly to the fact that people are afraid to walk the streets near the churches because of prostitutes and purse snatchers and partly thanks to high parking costs. In the old days, you could park free. Out-of-towners now report nightmarish experiences in which their cars are towed from lots by unscrupulous operators who then force them to pay sixty-dollar "towing fees."

State Senator Steven Perskie, a driving force behind the casino movement, admits casinos have brought problems. Transportation is bad, housing is scarce and expensive and local government is in danger of becoming controlled by casino interests. But, he told some Philadelphia reporters, "Most of these are the problems of development rather than the problems of stagnation we had before. Problems of development are solvable."

Others pointed out that you couldn't expect major changes overnight. Wait until there are more casinos, they said, until a lot more money is coming in, until the streets are no longer clogged with bulldozers and people don't awake to the din of construction at six in the morning. Already, they said, you could see the benefits. By late in 1978, Resorts had employed a hefty chunk of Atlantic City's unemployed, though most at menial, low-paying jobs. The high unemployment rate was not down, though, because of the numbers of people flooding into the area. It might go down when other casinos opened, unless continuing newcomers continued to make up the difference.

Another plus was that the construction industry was enjoying a boom. Also, the city was collecting higher taxes and the casinos were chipping in to local charities. (That was a practice that Resorts, for one, had not been renowned for in the Bahamas. The question was whether it would continue when casinos got the concessions they wanted from local groups.) Landowners, too, had benefited. The value of property had soared. Resorts International estimated that properties it had bought for $27 million were now worth between $600 million and $800 million, or one third the market value of all Atlantic City land.

But despite it all, many people were not sure that all of the progress was worth it. A long-time resident of Atlantic City wrote a letter to the Philadelphia *Bulletin*:

Where once it was possible to leave a front door open with no thoughts of being "ripped off" . . . to sleep on one's porch to beat the summer heat; to know, either directly or through the neighborhood grapevine, where one's children were and what they were doing; there is now only fear, mistrust and apathy.

The people, the lifeblood of this city, are being told they must leave in order that they may be replaced by a transfusion of new blood; a plasma of gold and silver. Those who have weathered the winters of desolation; who stayed behind and kept the Lady from being completely washed away—are being asked to cash in their chips and leave . . . Whole neighborhoods are being asked to move; to abandon with no forethought to the consequences other than a profit margin. Where once pride existed, there is only a slowly creeping tide of greed.

CHAPTER THIRTY

The press, through that first half year of casino, dutifully reported most of what happened. But in the midst of stories on the take and the drug program and the mob, there was one important event that went all but unrecorded. Dennis Gomes was gone. In September of 1978, he and his wife packed up, wrenched themselves away from their just-built home and went back to Nevada. Gomes said that investigation and enforcement in New Jersey was a sham that might result in big scandals. He didn't want to be a part of it.

For months there had been dribblings of dissatisfaction, hints that all was not peaceful, but Robert Martinez, director of the Division of Gaming Enforcement, pooh-poohed them when I asked him. He said you had to expect little grumblings from investigators; it was "the natural result of growing pains." But he told me not to pay too much attention to what they tell you.

The rumors continued: there was mutiny in the ranks, the division was understaffed and overworked, talented accountants were doing background checks on cocktail waitresses, there was confusion and disarray. The rumors turned out to be mostly true. By the fall, not only had Gomes quit, but so had one third of his Special Investigations Bureau. That bureau was disbanded.

At first the investigators wouldn't talk about it. They were scared—they didn't want to lose their jobs before they found new ones. Those who had already left were afraid that leaks would be traced to them and somehow they would suffer for it. One man wanted to talk, but said he couldn't: he had a wife and small children and couldn't afford to lose his job. "If I were a bachelor I'd do it," he said. "Hell, I'm a reckless sort of guy. But I don't think there's anything those people won't stop at to get a license." He added: "But I'll tell you what the investigation was like. Tie my hands behind my back and put me in a ring with Muhammad Ali. That's what it was like."

Eventually some did talk to me, and they painted a dismal portrait of New Jersey's attempt to police casinos. In the beginning of the Resorts investigation, they said, Dennis assigned his team to specific areas of study: financial stability, organized-crime associations, stock manipulation. It worked fine until Martinez started to meddle. Martinez thought Dennis was too secretive. He wanted to know everything that was going on when it was going on, and that wasn't the way Dennis worked. Dennis had been promised control of his investigations and free rein, and he expected the state to keep its promise. (A state official later countered, "There are no stars in New Jersey law enforcement.")

A lot of the guys at the SIB thought Martinez was jealous of Dennis. Everybody liked Gomes, but not many were fond of Martinez. They all agreed he was a great intellect, maybe even brilliant, but that didn't make him likable. Martinez was always trying to impress people. If someone said he liked to run, he would say he was a runner too. Then he would give some ridiculously low figure for how fast he could run a mile, and they would look at his physique and know it wasn't so.

They also thought he acted in peculiar and unprofessional

ways. He would show up in the morning with his clothes all rumpled, looking as if he had been out all night. He had a piece of scrap metal hanging in his office and he bragged that it was the fender from a state police car he had cracked up. One night he took some of the investigators on a tour of Trenton. He drove them through the red-light district and they all thought that was funny—the first time. But when he did it again and again, it made them nervous. They told him to stop, asked how it would look if someone spotted them. Another time, they said, he was drunk on the casino floor. They were afraid a Resorts official would see him and somehow use it against them. On a trip to Florida to interview Dino Cellini, Martinez tried to talk another investigator into going to Paradise Island with him and picking up women. That was almost sad, some investigators thought. It was as if he had some psychological need to get caught.

But Martinez's personality didn't matter as much as what was happening to the investigation. Late in the summer of 1978, when the Special Investigations Bureau was disbanded, all of its investigators became part of the mishmash of the Division of Gaming Enforcement. Martinez called a meeting of all the personnel of the division to announce the change. Some of Gomes' investigators protested, but to no avail. Gomes was effectively demoted, placed under a state trooper who, an investigator said, "was a great guy with lots of experience in blue-collar crime and almost none in white collar. He knew he needed Dennis."

Investigators were switched off topics they had been probing for months. Some were frustrated because, they said, their investigations were dropped just as they were beginning to prove rewarding. There was a probe to determine whether Resorts had paid off politicians to get the vote out on referendum day. It was "put on the back burner" by order of Martinez and never got started again. The state's answer, when officials were questioned later, was that it was a matter of judgment. They said investigators didn't realize that time and money could be better utilized elsewhere.

The shuffling of investigators often seemed to make no sense. Men with no accounting background were put on examinations of financial stability. Accountants were made to do wasteful checks on what one called "companies that supplied rubber bands to Resorts."

There was acrimony between state troopers and accountants. The troopers didn't like the fact that the accountants made more money. The accountants got sick of the troopers bragging that they could drive to Atlantic City at ninety miles an hour and never get a ticket.

Over twenty members—almost all—of what had been the SIB banded together to decide what to do. They were afraid to talk in the office, so they organized a baseball game and, said an investigator, "I think there was even a baseball or two lying around somewhere." The investigators came up with a plan. They would hire a lawyer and send him to talk to Attorney General Degnan. They would demand the removal of Martinez, and if he was not removed, they would go to the press. They decided, too, that if anyone from the SIB was fired, they would all quit and take the story of the farce of the investigation to the press.

They went to see a Trenton lawyer and asked his advice. He told them to forget it, they were crazy to even think of such a thing. He said the only investigators who could survive the aftermath of that move would be Dennis Gomes and the one or two others who had come from Nevada. They could go back to Nevada. The others would be fired and then blackballed from other jobs in New Jersey.

The investigators were dispirited. They decided that all that was left was to find jobs and quit one by one. A few left, then Dennis, which made spirits sink even lower. Said one disillusioned accountant, "Gomes was the only person who would stand up for us. Without him we became puppets." Eventually almost all of them left and reported that no one even debriefed them on what they had learned about Resorts in that year of investigation.

Dennis Gomes took an executive post at a Las Vegas casino, at a hefty increase in salary. He bought a fancy car and told himself he didn't care. He said Atlantic City was depressing anyway. Once when he was leaving the casino, he saw a young black kid of about eighteen running out. The kid had lost all his money, but it didn't bother him. He said as soon as he got some more he would be back. He knew how it worked now. Next time he would win. Gomes said that was what happened when you put a casino in the middle of a slum. At least with Las Vegas you had to cross a desert to get there.

Anyway, Dennis said, he was tired of law enforcement. He didn't like what it was making him become. When he worked in Nevada, his wife came home late one night from her job dancing. He was asleep, but he half woke and began to interrogate her—Where had she been? Who was she with? What were they doing?—like she was some casino manager. His wife was terrified. Another time in Atlantic City, he saw the look in an casino employee's eyes when he was interrogating him about lost chips; the man looked like an animal at bay. Dennis hated whatever it was in him that could not care when he made a man look like that.

There are three schools of thought on that Dennis Gomes move into the world of casinos. Some people think Gomes sold out, that by leaving and going to a casino he undid all the good. Others say not so, he gave it his best shot twice—once in Nevada, once in New Jersey. In the end he concluded, on more than a little evidence, that people got the law enforcement they deserved. He concluded they just didn't care. Why should he? The third school: Dennis Gomes was just one more of the inevitable casualties of gambling—proof that faced with the pressures of politics and the lure of fortunes, even the strongest and the smartest eventually succumb.

CHAPTER THIRTY-ONE

On Thanksgiving weekend 1978, there was a hastily called meeting of New Jersey law enforcement officials at the home of Attorney General John Degnan. The topic was the investigation of Resorts International, which was dragging on toward the one-year mark. The pressures to wrap it up were intensifying. Resorts was about to embark on the final three-month extension of its temporary license. The media was beginning to get wind of problems in the enforcement division and was implying that any recommendation but "no" would be a fix. The governor told the attorney general, "The best thing you can do is recommend they get a license. The next best thing is recommend they don't. Either way, get the damned investigation over with." The attorney general, when first told of the case against Resorts, supposedly said that he couldn't believe they had the nerve to apply in the first place.

What came out of the meeting struck like lightning on Monday, December 4. The New Jersey attorney general's office announced that as a result of the year-long investigation into Resorts International by the Division of Gaming Enforcement, it had seventeen exceptions to allowing the company to operate in Atlantic City. It recommended to the Casino Control Commission that Resorts be denied a permanent license.

It had been a difficult decision. If they decided in favor of Resorts, they risked charges that the investigation had been sabotaged. But then again, they had been hearing for months, ad nauseam, threats by the industry that if the state appeared too strict or too capricious in its enforcement, other operators would stay away. The officials wondered if they were setting standards that were too high. Should gambling companies be judged on the same basis as the rest of society?

They decided, in the end, that they had to move to deny the license, and their decision may have had less to do with all the philosophizing than it did with the fact that the press had given them no other choice. They could not leave themselves open to accusations that if Resorts could get into New Jersey, anybody could.

There had been hints it was coming, some public and some less so. First, the governor had visited Atlantic City only a week before the report was released and made unprecedented disparaging remarks about Resorts. He said that it never should have been allowed to open in what was nothing more than a renovation. He did not mention that he was one of the driving forces behind that speedy opening.

Also, I had heard the decision was coming from a former investigator. He said, "They're going to make a case of bad associations and they're going to make a case that Resorts had lousy controls in Paradise Island. But they're not going to come up with anything that will lose them their license. The way that investigation was run, how could they?"

When the seventeen "exceptions" were announced, Resorts was about to begin explaining away the problems of the first weeks to the commission. Those "problems" included the "embezzled" $180,000 and the lost $14,000 in chips. The state charged that Resorts had misrepresented its readiness to open. Resorts countered that no one could possibly have expected the kinds of crowds that converged on the casino. It claimed that it didn't report the lost $180,000 because it thought it was a "bookkeeping" problem. As to those hundreds of other violations, many having to do with unlicensed employees and the failure to follow proper procedures, Jack Davis said he had been worried about those too, but he said he got "assurances" from Robert Martinez one night in the baccarat pit. Davis said he told Martinez that he feared they could not follow the letter of the law. Davis' account of what happened then: "He [Martinez] said, 'Well, you have to do what you have to do, and if you commit some violations, you will, down the road a couple of months, get'—I don't remember if he said traffic violations or speeding tickets—'you'll get some minor discipline and it will all be in the past.' " Martinez never denied the story. Resorts was eventually fined—far less than the amount that was missing.

In its new report, the state's "exceptions"—findings that might constitute grounds to deny a license—included Mary Carter's dealings with Wallace Groves and Louis Chesler; Mary Carter's payments to a government official, Sir Stafford Sands, to get a gaming license; Mary Carter retaining the old Chesler-Groves staff even after those two had been discredited.

The state claimed that in opening the Paradise Island Casino, Mary Carter borrowed money from unsuitable characters, including several whose licenses to engage in the securities business were later revoked, suspended or denied because they manipulated the stock of Mary Carter Paint, and others who had been similarly disciplined or charged with banking and securities violations. They said that Mary Carter had lied to the Bahamian government when it held that it had fired Eddie Cellini. The state claimed that Resorts disassociated itself from a junket operator, James Neal, an alleged organized-crime figure, only when it became apparent that his association was about to become public, but they did not dismiss an employee,

Peter Hayes, part of the same Canadian mob group, because there was no threat of public exposure.

The state further charged that the Paradise Island Casino maintained a materially deficient system of accounting and internal controls, and that Resorts brought many of the same deficiencies with it to the Atlantic City casino.

They noted that Resorts International maintained an unrecorded cash fund from which it rendered payments to Bahamian public officials in return for what it described as "good-will" treatment: "This fund also utilized the Paradise Island Casino's marker [IOU] procedures for the issuance of payments, thus manifesting management's ability to manipulate the marker process."

The state further disapproved of Resorts employee Seymour Alter, who admitted an attempt to bribe a judge and who supplied paid female companions to Bahamian public officials. Finally, they claimed that David Probinsky, the PR man, was a friend of an individual of criminal association, Mike McLaney, and he was being paid a large salary and stock options to shut up.

Resorts reacted as if stung. James Crosby said it was all old stuff. He said there was nothing in the report the state didn't know before they granted the temporary license and that the state should have brought the charges before the company invested $77 million to "pioneer" in Atlantic City. Lawyer Joel Sterns rose at the commission meeting and demanded the "speediest" hearing because the state's charges were so "damaging." Commission chairman Joseph Lordi set a date, January 8, 1979. Lordi said, "The attorney general's report is only a report. The commission's determination will be based on testimony to be given before the commission."

Resorts' wrath increased when Attorney General John Degnan, in response to a question at a gathering of students, said that Resorts didn't deserve a license. He said he had been to

Las Vegas and was impressed by the controls there. He was dismayed by the "sloppiness" of Resorts. Resorts unleashed an angry press release accusing the attorney general of attempting to inflame public opinion. It said he had made statements that reached far beyond the division report. They thought he might be violating casino law in spirit, if not in fact, with his actions. Said Resorts: "We cannot and will not sit back and quietly accept this type of sensationalism on the part of the Attorney General. The character, reputation and integrity of the company and its principal officers have been impugned to an unbearable degree and on the basis of the weakest information."

Brendan Byrne, for his part, did not want to be caught on the wrong side of the fence. He was trying to polish up his white-knight image. He was a last-term governor, and it was rumored that he would be a Carter appointee to the post of U.S. attorney general. Most of the rumors were coming out of Trenton, not Washington. The problem was, a U.S. Senate committee report called an insurance company that Byrne had business ties to one of the ten worst in the country. Its salesmen used high-pressure telephone tactics and made false claims. It was not a good connection for a would-be U.S. attorney general to have. After the division report on Resorts came out, Byrne started making speeches about how New Jersey didn't need Resorts International. The state could find others to take its place.

CHAPTER THIRTY-TWO

For the upcoming licensing hearings, the state appointed a lawyer, G. Michael Brown, from its Division of Criminal Justice. Resorts hired a lawyer, Raymond Brown. About the only thing the two had in common was their last name, which would make following the hearings confusing. What they didn't have in common was style. Ray Brown had chewed up and spit out many a young lawyer before. Could he do it again?

There's a standing joke among New Jersey reporters: if you're innocent, get a lawyer; if you're guilty, get Ray Brown. Ray Brown operated out of Jersey City, a dingy little city in New York's backyard, and forged a reputation defending organized-crime figures. He liked to describe himself as a man who could afford to defend clients who needed him—often in civil-rights cases—at the expense of those who could afford to pay him, like Resorts International. His fee from Resorts for the short legal stint was said to be in six figures.

Raymond Brown is a brilliant criminal lawyer. To use a lesser word would be to do him an injustice. He is not the best educated, and certainly not the most intelligent. But as a tactician, he is all but unequaled in New Jersey. There is, for example, the way he uses his race. Raymond Brown is black.

You might not know it to look at him, but he'll tell you at the first opportunity. He makes his blackness an issue in almost every case he handles. He convinces juries that a vote against his client is a racist act—no matter the color of the client. He cleverly introduces into summations the idea that if his client is judged guilty, it is because his client's lawyer is black.

Ray Brown is full of theater, too, and fond of shenanigans, though he would probably never admit that's what they are. Once he was defending, on appeal, two men convicted of being Soviet spies. On the day he was to make his summation, he rushed into the courtroom late, wearing a U.S. Army colonel's uniform. He explained he had just come from Fort Drum military base. The inference was clear: Ray Brown stood for America and the flag; he would never defend anyone he really thought was a spy. His clients lost anyway.

Ray Brown has almost perfect pitch in determining which behavior is right for which courtroom and which case. His routine tends toward poor ol' country lawyer. He has a pronounced slouch, wears his clothes baggy, often speaks in self-deprecating tones. Then, when it's least expected, he pulls from nowhere an objection timed to ruin the moment of a prosecutor's line of questioning. Or he objects so often, and on such frivolous grounds, that opposing lawyers, often young, inexperienced state lawyers, become rattled, lose their train of thought, sometimes cave in. In New Jersey, they still talk about what he did to Sybil Moses.

Sybil Moses was the prosecutor in what was perhaps Ray Brown's most infamous case—the murder trial of Dr. X. "Dr. X" was the preindictment name *The New York Times* gave to Dr. Mario Jascalevich, a surgeon indicted on charges of murdering five patients at the former Riverdell Hospital in Oradell, New Jersey, in 1965–66 with injections of curare, a drug not easily detectable in the blood. Not only did Raymond Brown rip the state's case to shreds, he managed to make a media cause célèbre when he demanded that *Times* reporter Myron Farber hand over his notes. Farber ended up spending forty days in jail.

Raymond Brown also tore at prosecutor Moses. He called her a housewife and a schoolmarm and, some witnesses said, far less repeatable names. He objected countless times to questions she asked that were perfectly proper. He unnerved her and she reacted in the manner he had no doubt calculated—she lost her cool, fought back, stooped to his level. It was not the way to handle Ray Brown. Eventually, Dr. X was cleared of the charges. The state learned a lesson, which may have had something to do with its choice, for the Resorts International hearings, of its own—unrelated—Brown, G. Michael Brown.

Mickey Brown was a short, clean-cut, blond man in his early thirties with the solid square build of a wrestler. Mickey Brown could keep his cool when he had to and lose it when he meant to—for effect, but always in a controlled way. He would have lots of cause, against Ray Brown, to use the kind of "just anger" only God is supposed to have. Mickey Brown's reputation was that he was the state's best litigator, a man capable of thinking on his feet in a courtroom.

Mickey Brown had ably handled many a criminal case for the state's Division of Criminal Justice. But the Resorts hearings would be something different. Nobody was being tried for anything. There was no necessity to prove guilt, only unworthiness. Mickey Brown had to handle the evidence in a way that would show that there was enough that was damaging to prove Resorts did not deserve a license.

The state's lawyer confronted other obstacles. The case the Division of Gaming Enforcement was handing him was not tight. It might have been plenty if Resorts was not already running a casino, some experts thought, but it wouldn't be strong enough to get them thrown out. There were too many charges they could interpret themselves out of. And, too,

Mickey Brown might be fighting a preordained verdict. It was just possible that some, if not all, of the commissioners had already made up their minds.

On top of all of that, Mickey Brown had only a month to prepare. He was handed a report and given four short weeks to sort out the characters, subsidiaries, dates and places and to grope with sophisticated financial stuff that was out of his experience. So in mid-December Mickey Brown said goodbye to his very pregnant wife and holed up in a motel for a month of total immersion.

CHAPTER THIRTY-THREE

The incredible thing about Atlantic City that first week of hearings was that you couldn't get a room. When you walked down the Boardwalk, the frigid January air blasted sea mist and sand in your face from one side and steel splinters and stones and other construction debris from the other. It was so windy that people were grabbing on to the metal railing and pulling themselves along. But you couldn't get a room. It wasn't that the hearings generated such interest, but rather that the glass-and-china show was in town, one of the few big conventions left, and everything was booked solid.

Reporters from all over had to make do. I found a room with friends of a friend in Ventnor City, just a throw of the Monopoly dice down from Atlantic City proper. Others had to stay miles from town and commute each day. The hearings were in a gray old building in a room on the balconied second floor, looking down on the Miss America headquarters. There were loads of reporters there the first few weeks, everyone from Don Janson of *The New York Times* to Walt Tyminski of *Rouge et Noir* to Bruce Hallett of the New York *Daily News* to Lucinda Fleeson of the Bergen *Record* to the wire services to people from the U.S. Labor party selling a book that managed to link both Resorts International and Queen Elizabeth to the international drug trade. Local reporters were out in force too, and for the first couple of days it was press overkill because there was absolutely nothing to report on. The first day, Joseph Lordi, the commission chairman, gave a speech about how the hearings would be run and how each side would be heard and what the prevailing rules were. Ray Brown made his introductory remarks to the effect that it would be proven that Resorts was worthy. Mickey Brown made his opening speech about how Resorts had dealt with shady characters through the years not because they *had* to, but because they *chose* to.

Then it was down to business. Resorts would present its case first, with the state—Mickey Brown—having the option of cross-examining its witnesses, which it did in all cases. When Resorts rested, Mickey Brown would present whatever additional information the state had.

Once Ray Brown had begun his case, it didn't take reporters long to decide he was trying to bore them out of the room. Ray Brown didn't seem to like reporters much, maybe because they were often on the other side of his clients. That was particularly true in the case of Resorts, whose arrogance had not won it many friends in the press. During the hearings, though, Resorts exhibited an uncharacteristic concern for press relations. It hired reporter Phil Wechsler away from the New York *Daily News* and paid him a thousand dollars a week to handle reporters for the duration of the hearings. It lowered the fee later.

Phil Wechsler notwithstanding, the reason reporters thought they were being bored out of the room was that Ray Brown kept his witnesses talking about such things as parking facilities, banquet space, how many miles of conduit and piping there were in the Resorts hotel and whether the building was structurally pleasing. When they got to the part about the toilets being superior because they were imported from Italy, they really started losing their audience. Reporters decided it was a good time to catch up on gossip and stood in the back of the room or out in the hall, placing bets on whether Resorts would get a license.

The press was divided. Some said of course they would, they had spent scaddy-ad millions of dollars and supported all the right charities and greased all the right palms. It was too late to get them out, especially since they had been granted a temporary license. Others disagreed. They didn't think the commission could go against the attorney general the first time out. They said that while it would be nice if the state had more damning kinds of evidence, what they had should suffice. Almost everyone agreed that if Resorts was licensed, New Jersey would have to live with accusations that anyone could get in to Atlantic City, providing he or she could pay for it.

But reporters changed their opinions from minute to minute because the situation was not clear-cut. For example, the state criticized Resorts for employing Eddie Cellini. Some reporters thought Lordi was in an awkward position to make judgments on that one, since it was so similar to his own case. State police had recommended against the chairman in the "Lordi report" because, among other things, his family had business ties to the brother of a gangster. Could Lordi condemn someone in the same situation?

Another way reporters passed the time was guessing who was who in the audience. The hearing room was crowded. There was a roped-off section that reined in Resorts executives, their witnesses and other close to them. Jack Davis was there a lot, as were his right-hand man Steve Norton, Robert Peloquin, Pat McGahn, Joel Sterns and bachelor Crosby's young girlfriend. There was also an omnipresent middle-aged lady nobody could identify. Herb Wolfe, an ex-newspaperman turned temporary PR man, joked that she was Mary Carter. Everyone thought that was pretty funny. (It turned out that she was Crosby's sister.) The general-seating section was also chock full of Resorts supporters, some of whom worked for the company and appeared to be on paid holiday at the hearings. There were also a number of shareholders looking after their interests.

The first witness that anyone was interested in hearing was Richard Olsen, the Miami lawyer who matchmade Mary Carter and Huntington Hartford. Ray Brown led Olsen through a long, detailed account of how he had come to meet Crosby and Hartford and of early details of the transactions. It was pretty dry stuff. One moment worth sitting up for was when Ray Brown produced a memo written by two gaming investigators about their interview with Olsen. Olsen called it "the greatest mistatement of facts I have seen in twenty years of practicing law." Ray Brown said, "There's a reference here to the fact that Huntington Hartford's well-known sexual proclivities were mentioned by this man. It's in the report. He never did." It was an early attempt by Resorts to discredit the state's case. Much of what was in the memo was parenthetical. For example, there was a line that read, "Unexcelled was alleged to have been taken over by Crosby with the financial backing of Col. Gustave Ring (a suspected OC [organized-crime] figure from Washington, D.C.)." Olsen said he never said any such thing about organized crime. Mickey Brown told him it was parenthetical, meaning it was the observation of the memo writer. The discussion wasted plenty of time.

The next major witness was a surprise so early in the proceedings—James Crosby. It might have been a good move because he was an excellent witness, if you didn't count the numerous I-don't-knows and I-don't-remembers at crucial junctures. He was a combination of humor, self-deprecation, outrage, offense and, perhaps most important, sickness. There was no measuring the sympathy effect of the coughing, or the ten-minute breaks built into the program so he could take his oxygen, or the rumors that he was testifying so early because they thought he was going to die. He was frail and pale and looked like an old man, which he was not. Once when everyone was milling about during a break, Crosby came and leaned over the railing in the hall, just sort of hung there, seeming to gasp for breath. It was a pitiful sight except to those cynical enough to wonder why he was gasping there, not in the private Resorts quarters down the hall, and why no one was with him if he was so sick. Some wondered if it was a bald pitch for sympathy. Others sympathized.

Ray Brown led Crosby through his career, built him up as a superb businessman who knew a good acquisition when he saw one. Several times the point was made—in his and later testimony—that Crosby never liked the casino business. He had gotten involved only because it was the way to make money on Paradise Island. Another frequent tack was to put things off onto Jack Davis. Crosby often replied that he didn't know about something because "Jack was in charge of that." (In Jack's subsequent testimony, he similarly put much responsibility off on Robert Peloquin and Charles Murphy, and reporters wondered if Resorts was staging it so that if it was accused of wrongdoing, the buck would have been passed down to the bottom of the management ladder.)

Crosby admitted he dealt with Wallace Groves, even though he was a convicted felon, because Sir Stafford had told "a heartwarming story" about how Groves "had come out of a short stint in prison and had gone to the Bahamas and settled on a remote island and gone into the logging business, really to the point where he was, according to Sands, chopping the trees down himself and living in a tent for many years and that's how he came upon Freeport, actually." Crosby said Groves certainly seemed like he had rehabilitated himself.

Crosby talked about the various people who had been involved in early Resorts "private placements" of stock. The suitability of many of these people was called into question by Gaming Enforcement because after the private placements, quite a few became embroiled in controversy. One was William Mellon Hitchcock, a wealthy heir whom the SEC later accused, along with others, of manipulating the stock of Mary Carter Paint. (A number of these people signed consent decrees, which means, in Wall Street parlance, they denied they did anything wrong but promised they wouldn't do it again.) He was also convicted, in 1973, of violating federal banking laws. Another buyer was Frank Mace, who the division claimed was holed up at the Ocean Club when he was wanted by the SEC. Two others were financier Bernie Cornfeld, with his Fund of Funds money, and Burt Kleiner, of Kleiner Bell in Beverly Hills, who was later barred from the securities business for life.

Crosby described each entity, some of whose names were hidden by their company name or the fund they ran. There were some Greek twins from the Goulandris family—the richest of all the Greeks, he thought. There were some mutual funds and some local people from Paradise Island, like the daughter of the chairman of the board of the "21" Club in New York. In the middle of describing one of the people, Crosby had an outburst: "That's why I'm so distressed about this implication that there is something improper about this— because I handled it. If there is something wrong, it is wrong with me, and every one of those people were the type of people I thought then and I still think now were the kind of people that should have been buying stock."

Ray Brown cut him off and put him back on the track. After they finished the list, Ray Brown asked Crosby if he had ever dealt with Louis Chesler after the initial Groves-Chesler casino dealings. Ray Brown obviously realized that the state would have liked to prove that Resorts did business with Chesler *after* Sir Ranulph Bacon's 1967 Royal Commission of Inquiry report looked askance at Chesler-Groves. Crosby said no, they had not. The question plucked a string in my mind. I remembered hearing about a Paradise Island real estate deal in the late sixties between Chesler and Resorts. I made a note to make some calls.

Crosby's testimony went on for days. The high point of most days was lunch, when reporters who weren't rushing to make deadlines gathered at local hamburger joints to decide who was ahead in the hearings. One restaurant, Little John's, was built into an old church, and the hamburgers had names like Sir Bacon burger, which everyone insisted on calling Sir Ranulph Bacon burger when they were ordering. You had to be there.

One day at lunch I called a friend in Florida and asked him if he remembered a Chesler-Resorts real estate deal on Paradise Island. Of course, he said. In 1969, Chesler was going to put up some condominiums on the shores of Paradise Lake. A model was built right by the bridge (which Sy Alter eventually ended up living in) and there was a big party thrown for the opening of the model. Later on, the deal collapsed because the real estate recession hit, my source thought. I asked if he had any proof—old promotion circulars, anything. It would really be going out on a limb to print what may have been a perjury by Crosby without airtight proof. He said he would look.

When I called him later, he had come up with a 1969 financial report which stated that a Canadian company (it didn't say who, true to Resorts form) had purchased six acres of land on Paradise Island and was building condominiums. The source said the Canadian company was either Residential Resorts or Roberts Realty, both of which were Chesler outfits. He said, too, that he had called several people in Nassau and Paradise Island and asked if they remembered a condominium project; they all said, "Oh, sure, you mean that Lou Chesler deal."

When I eventually printed the story, it caused Resorts some heat. Al Merck brought it up and so did Mickey Brown, but Resorts deflected it. They said of course they remembered the project, it was an *Alan* Chesler project. Alan was the son of Louis. Charlie Murphy said there was never a model built and never an opening party—untrue. Nobody pushed further.

It was stories like that that put me on the list of what must have been the five reporters Resorts most disliked. The problem was that *Barron's* affected them where it hurt the most—in their stock price. Following negative stories in *Barron's* on Resorts—and other companies, too—the stock price often went down. Needless to say, though, in those early days of the Resorts casino, it never stayed down long. They needn't have worried.

Early in the Atlantic City hearings, Resorts' new PR man, Phil Wechsler, was cold toward me, even though we had met before under friendly circumstances. It seemed now that Resorts had indicated the enemy, and I was part of it. I joked with Wechsler at the hearings, and eventually he became civil, even friendly. I would ask him, "Hey, Phil, when's Resorts gonna confess?" and he would laugh and say, "Any minute now, Crosby's gonna tell the one about Lansky and everything."

One day during an intermission, I was chatting with Wechsler in the hearing room. His back was toward the door and I knew he didn't see Jack Davis walk in and look at us. I kept talking and laughing and trying to look like it was a cordial conversation. Then Phil happened to glance over and notice Davis, and his whole demeanor changed. He physically stepped back from me a foot or more and the smile vanished from his face. He looked like he was going to run away, but he caught himself, said a few more words, much more somber than before, and walked away. It eventually got to the point where if I called him with a question, he would reply with an icy "No comment."

Other Resorts people were good at spotting their "enemies." I sat most days with Bruce Hallett, from the *Daily News,* and we were usually next to or in the general vicinity of Tom

Cannon, the attorney general's press man, and PR man Herb Wolfe. Almost every day the same sort of odd couple sat behind us. She was matronly, an Atlantic City resident, a woman who chattered nonstop. He was a big, brawny young man whose chest strained against his tightly tapered shirt. He was as slick-looking as she was motherly.

She began striking up conversations with reporters. She worked for Resorts, she said, had once been in personnel but wasn't anymore. She wasn't saying where she was. He didn't say much, looked like he might be a dealer in the casino. He was always making sarcastic remarks like, "Hey, did you hear who the big surprise witness is gonna be today? It's Meyer Lansky!" (He wasn't that far off the mark on what the press might believe. Someone started a rumor that Stafford Sands was at Resorts International and there might be a Pulitzer in it for the reporter who interviewed him. If so, it would have been the first Pulitzer given to a reporter who interviewed a man who had been dead for ten years.) She wanted to know who all the reporters were and where they came from.

By the second week she had figured out who she was not supposed to like. High on the list were commissioner Al Merck, Walt Tyminski, Tom Cannon and me. She would sit behind any or all of us and discourse loudly on how wonderful Resorts was, it had brought young people back to Atlantic City, it was bringing money to Atlantic City. Her speech got louder and more pointed as the days wore on, and I wondered if she was a Resorts "plant" and if there were others like her around the room whispering not-so-sweet nothings in other reporters' ears. She said she was tired of all these reporters. Who did they think they were, criticizing these nice boys at Resorts? And that Al Merck, always asking terrible questions, he ought to be thrown off the commission.

Once during a break, I was sitting reading when she and her sidekick sat behind me. She all but screamed that now-familiar theme—How dare all these awful people try to hold things against Resorts that they had done ten years before? Who cared if they dealt with the mob? Who cared if they paid off a few government officials? They should be forgiven, they shouldn't have to put up with this outrage, because they took the chance, they came to Atlantic City first and they should be let in despite everything or anything that had gone before. I sat through about five minutes of it, then stood up, turned and faced her. What I wanted to say was "You're right! Let's get Hitler in here and give him a license too!" But I didn't. I simply moved to a quieter section of the room and continued my reading.

Back at the Crosby testimony, there was a revelation: a new Probinsky contract, dated January 6, 1979. It had been inspired by Gaming Enforcement's criticisms of the old contracts. Crosby said they had arranged to pay Probinsky up front so nobody would think he was being muzzled. But it wasn't quite true. He was indeed being paid a discounted $400,000 instead of the sums over ten years originally agreed upon, but that amount and his stock were still being held in escrow until Resorts received its license. Crosby explained that the reason Probinsky got a contract in the first place was that he was always criticizing everyone else in the company. "I don't know why it is so extraordinary that you should ask somebody that is working for you not to do anything detrimental to the company that he is working for," Crosby exclaimed.

Crosby went on to defend Resorts' large political contributions in the Bahamas as "traditional." He also said that Sy Alter had been suspended in December after the division report revealed he had tried to bribe a judge. Crosby said he had no prior knowledge of the attempted bribe. (When questioned on the same subject in December, Davis at first said he had no knowledge of it. The next day, when he was forced to recant, he said he had known and had been temporarily confused when the first reporter asked.)

On day five of the Crosby testimony, Ray Brown produced a letter from a Bahamian law firm which stated that under Bahamian law, it was legal to make contributions to political parties and candidates. The law firm was the successor to Stafford Sands' firm. Shortly after, Ray Brown rested. Mickey Brown was at bat, and now Ray Brown could show some of the defensive antics that earned him his reputation.

There were two immediate ploys. The first was that when Mickey Brown asked a controversial question, Ray Brown would either object or interrupt in some other way, especially when it looked like his client was at a temporary loss for an answer. Brown's interruptions were probably designed to addle Mickey Brown and to warn the client that he was on tender ground, but rarely were they based on any valid points of law.

One day, for example, Mickey Brown asked Crosby, of a man with whom a sale had been negotiated, "Who is he?" Crosby began, "He is a young man . . . how should I describe him? I don't know how to describe him." Ray Brown piped up: "Was he tall or short?" The focus of the room turned toward Ray Brown, Mickey Brown temporarily lost his train of thought and Crosby had time to prepare his answer. Another time, Mickey Brown used the name Dino instead of Eddie Cellini, and though he immediately recognized the mistake and apologized, Ray Brown jumped all over him and kept pushing the subject until finally Lordi said "Come on, gentlemen" and broke it up.

The second ploy Ray Brown used was to position himself so that he had eye contact with his witness-client Crosby and could coach him with nods and shakes of the head and other signals. When Mickey Brown figured out what was going on, he moved the podium he was using so that it blocked that eye contact. That afternoon, Robert Peloquin, who had been in the audience, pulled a chair into the front area of the room, where only the commissioners and the witness sat. It was as if a spectator in a court trial opened the gate into the front section and pulled his chair into the middle of the trial area. No one objected. Peloquin took over the coaching of Crosby, bobbing and shaking his head like one of those miniature football players on people's dashboards.

There was little in the state report that Resorts denied, but they cast everything into a different light. Their most frequent defense was that none of the people they dealt with who were indicted, who were forced to sign consent decrees or who turned out to be connected to organized crime surfaced in a bad light until *after* Resorts dealt with them. Crosby said he thought all of the people to whom he sold stock were fine people and that there was no way to know that some of them would try to manipulate it. He said that it was not until articles in *Life* magazine that he knew he had to sever relations with Groves and Chesler. He had not known before that they were tied to the mob.

By the middle of the second week of testimony, it looked like the state was losing ground. Mickey Brown was not making his points clearly. He often didn't follow up on important lines of questioning, dropping them when they seemed at the moment of revelation. He had very little flair for the dramatic. And, too, his lack of time for preparation was showing. Temperamentally, though, he was a good match for Ray Brown. He kept calm, most of the time, his eyes constantly prowling the hearing room. But some days—for example, one where Ray Brown's objections and interruptions were so plentiful that counters lost track at sixty—the effect was plain to see. Mickey Brown was rattled.

It was not that the state did not have plenty that should have at least put some sweat on Crosby's brow. There was, for example, a commission of $730,000 paid by Resorts to a man named Richard Gittlin for arranging a $1.75 million loan to Resorts from American National Life Insurance Company of Galveston. (American National has been a controversial company because, contrary to most guidelines of what constitutes proper disposition of insurance-company funds, it has often made loans to controversial casinos.) Mickey Brown wondered what the man had done to deserve a commission of over 40 percent. Crosby said he had arranged the loan quickly. But the plot thickened. Gittlin had been cited in a memo to Intertel from one of their outside sources as a rumored associate of Meyer Lansky. Intertel apparently either ignored or discounted the allegation. Also, the transaction was handled at the insurance-company end by a vice-president, Fred Blencowe, who left not much later to join Gittlin at his firm, Republic Funding. Blencowe later showed up on the board of directors of Crosby's old firm, Unexcelled Chemical. It was a peculiar sequence of events, but Mickey Brown never questioned hard enough or far enough to force Crosby to explain it. It was one of many such instances.

On another occasion, Mickey Brown spent the better part of one session discussing a point of Probinsky's new contract that turned out not to exist. He had misunderstood the terms.

Commissioner Al Merck, true to form, was more probing, much to Chairman Lordi's frequently exhibited disgust. Merck had asked a couple of reporters to supply him with questions because he felt the press might be better versed than he. Someone suggested he ask about the Huntington Hartford-Resorts buy-out deal. The Bank of Commerce, over Hartford's protest, had sold his shares of Island Hotel Company, the subsidiary that owned the Paradise Island Hotel, for $20,000 to the only bidder, Resorts, which then turned around and valued it on its own books at $897,000. Merck said that unlike the other commissioners, he was sophisticated about corporate dealings. He was a director of Merck Pharmaceuticals, after all.

But when his turn came, he blew it on that question and others. He got the shares mixed up with some shares Hartford owned in Resorts, the discussion went on confusingly for a few minutes, then Merck seemed to get embarrassed and dropped it.

Reporters had all but begged Merck to ask who the secret owners of the Paradise Island Bridge were, and he did. Crosby named Gerald Goldsmith, a businessman in the Bahamas, and the Cosmos Bank. Merck asked who was in the Cosmos Bank. Crosby said it included Frederick Glass, who was the head of the Air Transport Command and was a counsel to American Airlines; a former president of Switzerland; and then head of one of the big Wall Street law firms, successor to a Secretary of State. (The last one stunned me. I had known the man for fifteen years. I had seen him three or four times since I had written my first articles on Resorts, and he took every opportunity to verbally attack me for the stories. Never once did he admit to being a part owner of the bridge.) Crosby added that neither Rebozo nor Nixon was a bridge shareholder.

Merck asked Crosby why Sy Alter, sitting on the executive floor of a multimillion-dollar corporation, would be assigned to the job of hiring cocktail waitresses. (The Division of Gaming Enforcement and the local A.C.L.U. had received some complaints that Alter was making sleeping with Resorts executives a precondition of employment.) Crosby said Alter was in charge of special projects and, under questioning, added that he had never heard any complaints about Alter and cocktail waitresses.

On Friday, January 19, at lunchtime, Crosby stepped down from the witness stand for good. Next up would be Jack Davis. From the looks of things, the hearings would drag on for months.

CHAPTER THIRTY-FOUR

In mid-January, as the hearings plodded along in New Jersey, Florida authorities found Donna Wilson, Crosby's once girl-friend, who they believed—and they are probably wrong—was a "baglady" for Resorts. She was living in southern Florida. A couple of men from the New Jersey Division of Gaming Enforcement traveled to Miami and, together with members of the Florida Department of Public Safety, interviewed her. Following that interview, the New Jersey investigators asked Donna Wilson to fly to New Jersey to talk some more. She went, was asked more questions, then was told her testimony was unusable because she had been Crosby's mistress.

The record of Donna Wilson's interview does not read like that of a woman scorned. She said she had decided to talk because her mother convinced her it was the right thing to do. She seemed genuinely fond of Crosby; she didn't want to hurt him, she said, but she didn't think he knew half the things Peloquin and Davis and the others were pulling off. Sometimes when the state asked her leading questions, she would say, "Now, see, I don't know anything about that." A bitter person might have gone along with the line of thought to make the company look bad. Donna Wilson did not. What she said was as credible as the testimony of the parade of Resorts' witnesses up in New Jersey who had a vested interest in the hearing's outcome, but the state didn't call her to testify in front of the commissioners and they never mentioned her deposition to the commission.

Donna Wilson first came to Paradise Island through Huntington Hartford, as her story went: "There used to be an A and P grocery store behind where I lived in Detroit, and I heard [Hartford] had gotten a divorce from his wife, so I went to New York and called him up and said, 'Hi, I'm new. I just moved here and I know you have a lot of connections, so do you think you could help me find a job and an apartment?' So he was going to get me into the modeling business, but that was too long and I needed an immediate job. I took a job at the Waldorf-Astoria waiting on tables, and he used to baby-sit for my son. Then I went down to the Bahamas and stayed at his house, plus then I met Sy Alter . . . I went down to Nassau and tried to stay for as long as I could. I liked it."

She met Crosby not quite a year later. "I met him once at Hartford's house and we all had dinner together, Crosby and Sy and a bunch of other people. But then I didn't see him again for a long time. He never remembered me, anyway. He was always drunk. Every time he kept getting introduced to me, he'd say, 'You're a beautiful girl, why haven't I met you before?' I'd say, 'Because you're too drunk to remember.' "

Eventually she became his girlfriend for five years, she said, and was his companion every night except when he was out of town. She often traveled with him to Miami and New York.

To make a living in the islands, Donna Wilson gambled for Bahamian residents, who, by law, were not allowed to gamble. She would take a 10 percent cut of the winnings. One of her "clients," Sy Alter, gave her a big cut—a couple of hundred dollars each time.

Investigators asked Donna Wilson about a trip she took to

New York with Peloquin. She explained: "I went up there, went to the Pierre Hotel and met a narc there—I can't remember his name anymore—and I went up with him [Peloquin] . . . We sat and parked on the West Side and watched somebody make a drop or pickup or something, some sort of small-time dope thing, and then I went into the club and I was supposed to find out—they were also bringing in this girl, too, who is an agent, but nothing was happening."

The questioners asked if the narcotics agents were there at the request of Peloquin. "Yes," she said. "I didn't see the girl, though. She never showed up, because there was nothing happening. When I went to the Show Club, there was no more drug deals, it was dead. I failed my mission."

"What was the purpose of your mission?" a questioner asked.

"To discredit Hartford."

"Can you explain how?"

"By proving he was involved with drugs or his club [the Show Club] was a big sort of dealing place."

"Was Peloquin behind the attempt to discredit Hartford . . . ?"

"Yes, they all were."

"Who is 'they all'?"

"I mean they all were in on it, Crosby and Sy and them, because when they sent me up there, everyone from Intertel, they were down in Nassau and they were giving me the first degree—my whole background, my life story. Before they sent me out, they asked me if I knew about drugs and had all these pictures of different pills and things like that . . . This is when Hartford was suing them . . . They were trying to get him back."

The investigators asked her if anyone from Resorts had contacted her. She replied, "Peloquin. The last three days, he's been calling."

"Why do you think Peloquin was trying to contact you now?"

"I don't know. I hung up on him."

Donna Wilson claimed that Resorts once asked her to do them a favor in return for a work permit, which they knew she wanted badly. Sy Alter asked her to go to the Jockey Club in Miami, pick up a box, bring it back and leave it on the plane, where it would be picked up. She was scared because she thought it was guns, but she said she would do it. They told her they would let her know when, but they never did. She never got her work permit, either.

Wilson said she was given a lot of other odd jobs by Resorts. "There was a lot of casino rip-offs going on, and they wanted me to infiltrate and find out how it was being done. They were losing a lot of money, like a million dollars or something really ridiculous . . . Crosby was very impressed that I came up with a lot of stuff, and that's when I warned them of the strike, the wildcat strike, and that's when they started firing one dealer after another, until they wound up firing about a hundred dealers."

She was asked what part she played: "Finding out who was doing it, who was head of whatever—you know, they had agents and all sorts of things—and getting them to inform, to have meetings with Peloquin, and he in turn guaranteed green cards for a lot of these guys. Some of the biggest thieves up there, all have green cards, and they own restaurants in Washington and New York." (She was referring to the cards aliens must have to allow them to work in the United States.) She claimed Peloquin was getting green cards for the ex-dealers, setting them up in businesses and taking a part of their profits.

She said she worked for Intertel for a while. They paid her $150 a week initially but later raised it to $200. She said that Hartford was always sending detectives down to see what they could find out. One detective came and wanted to talk to her, but Resorts said "No way. Then I went over with Peloquin, I went to Ed Dixon's house [Dixon was the man from whom Resorts bought Chalk's airlines] and made the phone call to Hartford and recorded it."

"What was the relationship between Ed Dixon, Peloquin and Intertel?"

"Well, Peloquin was Ed Dixon's lawyer. Ed was busted for income tax and everything else." She said Peloquin was a good lawyer because Dixon "only had to stay six months in jail, and for every month he was in jail he saved a million dollars that he would have had to pay the government."

Someone wondered if she knew of any gambling going on outside the casino on Paradise Island. She said they had poker games but that they would never let her in on them.

"Do you know any of the participants in these games?"

"No. I just know Sy Alter and Jack Davis always sat in, and they went in. Tom Blum knows, but he's not talking."

Tom Blum was the manager of the bridge on Paradise Island. He was fired because he had been caught with drugs and, according to Crosby, a gun. (There was another similar story. A casino manager who was liked by the Bahamian government but supposedly not by Resorts was almost busted for drugs when cops found a plastic bag full of marijuana in his car on Paradise Island. But they also found fingerprints on the bag belonging to a local boy who worked for Resorts. He was later arrested, admitted to the plant, but went to jail rather than say who had put him up to it.)

The investigators asked Donna Wilson if anyone told her to keep her mouth shut.

"Yes, Tom did. Tom Blum . . . He said this would be my big chance to get paid off, and I'd be an idiot to say anything . . . They were supposed to buy me a bar, and that would have been about two hundred thousand dollars. Of course they never did."

"Was this prior to the hearings which are now in progress?"

"Uh-huh."

"They didn't make the statement that 'we'll buy you this bar if you don't talk to any commission members'?"

"No. I guess maybe . . . they were stringing me along."

The investigators asked who had made reference to the bar. She said Blum, Peloquin and Crosby.

"How long ago did Blum say this was your chance to really get paid off?"

"Last night." Blum, she said, had been promised twenty thousand dollars. Also, Blum had a lot of stock in Resorts and didn't want to see it go under. Blum was given orders by Resorts on what he could and could not say to investigators: "They gave him a ten- or fifteen-page memorandum about what to say before he was questioned by you people." She said Crosby gave the memo to Blum.

They asked her, "Do you know of anyone else who got told not to talk to commission members?"

"No, because they got rid of me really fast, so I'm not in contact with anyone. They were in a real hurry to get rid of me. They wanted me to pull my son out of school in the middle of a term and ship my stuff over. They wanted to give me a couple of days and I wanted to find a decent area, and they said that once I get over there I could find another place. I'm not a gypsy, I can't keep moving."

"When did this happen?"

"This summer."

"Do you personally have any feelings on why they wanted you out?"

"They just wanted to get rid of me, that's all."

"Because of the things that you know?"

"No, I don't think that's why they wanted to get rid of me, but I think that's why they didn't want me found."

A new subject: Robert Vesco. The investigators told

Donna that Resorts officials said they were never involved with Vesco again after he was indicted. Did she know if it was true? She said it wasn't: "He was over at Crosby's house regularly, having meetings . . . I guess up until the time he went to Costa Rica."

"But you have no knowledge of what went on at these meetings?"

"They would never allow me. It was always 'Get lost.' "

"You never got to know [Vesco] personally?"

"Oh, yes. I flew down on his plane and everything. I used to hang out with his kids . . ."

"He was, from what I know," said one of the investigators, "given virtually free run at Paradise Island. Is that true?"

"Yes."

"He was a nonpaying guest?"

"No, he had his own house and he was a big tipper and a big gambler, so . . . I really couldn't say he was nonpaying."

"I have heard something to the effect that he may have had something to do with the bridge company or an interest in Resorts."

"See, that I don't know."

"Have you heard that he was, at one time, negotiating with Resorts to buy Paradise Island?"

"Yes, everyone thought he had bought it already."

"Do you know whether or not he ever did?"

"No. He was indicted. He couldn't do it because they [Resorts] are on the American Stock Exchange. The money was no good."

Another topic: "Do you know personally [that politicians] were on the payroll?"

"I never saw their paychecks, but I know they were on the payroll because Crosby was always in a fit and threatened to take them off the payroll because he was getting so much grief."

"These were local Bahamians?"

"Yes."

"Did you ever hear anything about any politicians from here?"

"No. I know they wined and dined the whole FBI and congressmen and everyone else from New Jersey. They had them all down—I don't know, congressmen, whatever . . . Resorts picked up the bill."

"Do you have firsthand knowledge?"

"I don't have the receipts, once again, but yes, I know for sure that's the thing. I didn't take notes and collect things. I didn't think I would ever have to use them. I should have, I suppose. I was going to wait for Crosby to die before I ever opened my mouth because I never wanted to hurt Crosby."

"Just because of this affection for him?"

"Uh-huh, but I have no affection for anybody else."

"Along those lines, do you feel you have been used by Resorts or Intertel or anyone?"

"I don't know. I have mixed emotions."

So ended the Florida testimony of Donna Wilson. Two former New Jersey investigators, when told about it, separately had the same reaction: So that's what happened when we went to see Tom Blum. They said that when the division had first approached Blum, by phone, he said he knew plenty and was willing to talk. By the time investigators got to Florida to meet with him, he had turned from a canary into a parrot, spouting the company line. They figured that somebody must have gotten to him before they did. They were both incredulous that the state had not used the Donna Wilson testimony. They thought it might have made all the difference.

A couple of weeks later, I was in Florida on business and mentioned to a law enforcement official in Miami that I was thinking of trying to see Donna Wilson. He said, "Listen, if you want to, go ahead, but let me warn you of one thing. Her house is being watched twenty-four hours a day, and we don't know by whom. We've narrowed it down to two—Intertel or the mob."

I didn't go.

CHAPTER THIRTY-FIVE

Back in New Jersey, the parade of witnesses marched on. Ray Brown asked Jack Davis about dealings with Louis Chesler, and Davis was well prepared to answer. He said Resorts had dealt with him in 1966, but never again. They had subsequent dealings with his son. He said, "Louis Chesler, I was told by Alan, had nothing to do with this operation, and in fact, it always seemed that the father and the son had very little desire to become involved in each other's business ventures." Which did not explain why the deal they made in 1966 was with both Alan *and* Lou, by Resorts' own admission. No one asked.

Brown asked Davis what Alter's job was at Resorts, and Davis said he was a consultant in the beginning. He helped in their dealings with Hartford and helped find employees through his many friends in the Bahamas. One of the employees he found was Steve Norton. (Steve Norton was one of the few, if not the only, Resorts executives whose background was not detailed before he was questioned in the hearings. Norton had come from the King's Inn, a hotel-casino on Freeport that was run by Morris Lansburgh, who later pleaded guilty to conspiring to skim profits from a Las Vegas casino to avoid taxes. Authorities thought the skim was a Lansky job.)

Davis was not the witness Crosby was. For example, one day he was asked if Henry and Charles Murphy were related. He said he *thought* they were cousins. He had known both of them for more than ten years. One was on his board of directors, the other was his chief legal counsel. Yet he *thought* they were cousins.

Another time, he was asked by Mickey Brown who had done the legal work on a certain transaction. Davis started to sidestep the question, then said he didn't know. He said, "It's a technical question. I could presume a guess." Mickey Brown said, "I'm not trying to be technical, I ask you as the chief operating officer." Raymond Brown sprang from his seat and objected to Mickey Brown's inference. Ray Brown said, "Either a person knows or he doesn't know." Mickey Brown said that Davis had described himself as the "chief operating officer." Raymond Brown said, "Of course, that's his position." Mickey Brown started to speak and Ray Brown cut him off: "My father cleans sewers. He was never addressed as Sewer Brown except at home. It doesn't make any sense."

Lordi said, "Answer the question." Davis said, "The best way I can answer is, I don't know." The hearing room burst out laughing.

There was other comic relief in Davis' testimony. He was asked whether a man named James Neal, an organized-crime figure, had run junkets to Paradise Island, as the division alleged. Davis said that they would have to ask Peloquin. He was then asked if he knew Neal in any other context. Davis said, "Yes, I met him once. He wanted to advise us on our laundry construction." The press giggled at the double meaning they found in that one.

Davis also admitted he had made "disbursements" to Bahamian officials by taking money out of the casino. That became an issue after the hearings were over, when it was divulged that a Bahamian government official had only recently been given a few-thousand-dollar "loan" to pay his son's tuition. Both examples pointed up the ease with which money left that casino.

Al Merck questioned Davis about a poem "On Loyalty," by Elbert Hubbard, appearing in the Resorts October 1978 in-house publication. It read:

If you work for a man, for heaven's sake work for him. Speak well of him and stand by the institution he represents. Remember, an ounce of loyalty is worth a pound of cleverness. If you must condemn and eternally find fault, resign your position and when you are on the outside, damn to your heart's content. But so long as you are a part of the company, do not condemn it. If you do, the first high wind that comes along will blow you away, and you will never know why.

Merck handled the question badly. He asked Davis, "Do you know what the expression 'blow you away' means in the underworld?" It got a fast objection from Ray Brown, who called it a cheap shot. Merck apologized, Davis said, "We will refrain from poetry in the future," and Lordi opened his questioning by calling Davis Crosby. Alice Corsey said, "It's Davis." Lordi said, "I mean Mr. Davis. That joke really got me, Al." The point that was lost was that it looked like Resorts was threatening people out of talking to investigators.

While Davis was on the stand, there was an interesting development in the outside world. Sy Alter's house was robbed by two men with stocking masks and phony French accents. Alter was not home at the time, but his wife was forced, at knife-point, to open his safe. The burglars took cash, jewelry and papers. The crime was never solved.

After Davis came Probinsky, who told his story colorfully, but not in a way that would endanger his million-plus dollars.

Lawyer Charlie Murphy took the stand and didn't bother to disguise his contempt for the proceedings. Old ground was covered, though under questioning by Mickey Brown there was one new development. Murphy was asked about transactions with William Mellon Hitchcock, the stockbroker who was later suspended for manipulating the stock of Mary Carter Paint. The division said Hitchcock had told them he thought that a certain transaction Resorts was involved in was handled by J. J. Frankel, a mob figure. Murphy said it wasn't true Hitchcock had told the investigators that, and he had a tape to prove it. Mickey Brown demanded the tape be produced. Murphy said he would be glad to, but under later questioning he said of the tape, "I tried to listen, but I couldn't make much sense out of it, personally, but I don't know. I could break a recorder quicker than I could make it play correctly." The tape was never produced, at least not publicly.

Murphy was questioned on why Resorts had not sued the many publications that had written negatively on it. His reply: "You don't slap every fly that lands on you."

Next on the list was Raymond Gore, senior vice-president for finance. His was a sweaty testimony—he was visibly nervous. A lot of the questioning centered on loose controls in the Paradise Island Casino. Gore said they were being upgraded (eleven years after opening, it might be noted). Questioned on a list of disbursements—political and charitable contributions —Gore guessed which were which. After a few guesses, he was asked, "You could determine whether it's charitable or not by the amount you gave?"

"Generally."

"If it is a low amount, you could assume that it is charitable?"

"Right."

Following Gore came Arthur Mathews, a lawyer with Wilmer, Cutler and Pickering in Washington. He was formerly with the SEC and he was at the hearings to testify that it was unfair to judge someone just because they had been forced to sign a consent decree with the SEC. Resorts had signed such a decree when the SEC charged it with lack of full disclosure during the attempted Pan Am takeover. Mathews said a lot of innocent people sign consent decrees because it is too expensive to fight them.

Mickey Brown cleverly introduced a speech Mathews gave at a bar association meeting in which he said, "I honestly and sincerely don't think that I have ever recommended settlement to a client in an injunctive case except in cases where I thought the client would lose on the merits. I think in the overwhelming amount of cases, the SEC does 'have the goods' on the client." Mathews said he had changed his mind.

Next up, Robert Peloquin. Again, repetition, long discussion of Intertel, how Crosby had come to Justice, what Peloquin had done at Justice. He had often investigated illegal and legal gambling, he said. He was stationed in Kentucky in the sixties, when illegal casinos were rampant there. He recalled that in the town of Covington, a famous ex-football player who was running for sheriff (on an anti-gambling platform) "got drugged and put in an embarrassing position by the town fathers so he would not appear to be a proper candidate for sheriff. They drugged him in Cincinnati, took him across the river into Newport, Kentucky, put him in the Glen Hotel, took his clothes off and had one April Flowers, an exotic dancer, present in the room with him."

Peloquin was cut off by Lordi, who demanded to know the relevance of the story.

Ray Brown said, "Life is short, Mr. Chairman."

Lordi said, "I knew that before I ever sat down in this chair."

Peloquin didn't finish the story, but later he talked about how morality changes and how nobody minded the illegal

ly not retracted anything and that he stood by every word
he story. But then he said that Peloquin had called him,
lained that Intertel was in danger of losing an important
nt because of the article and asked the publisher to send
a letter of retraction for his one client's eyes only. Green-
n says he agreed to do so if Peloquin promised never to use
letter elsewhere. Peloquin agreed, said Greenspun, and the
er was written. But it was used elsewhere, on many occa-
s, including when it was entered into the record in the New
ey hearings.

eloquin called Alan Witwer, the author of the article, "a
wn blackmailer." He said that Witwer had tried to black-
J. Edgar Hoover. He had gone around telling everybody
Hoover had taken freebies at a hotel Witwer worked at
alifornia. It took Al Merck, later in the proceedings, to ask
obvious question: "How can you blackmail someone when
go around broadcasting that you are going to blackmail
n?" Said Peloquin, "Oh, Mr. Hoover thought he was being
kmailed." Peloquin also referred to Norman Casper, the
informant-detective from Key Biscayne, as having been
er "charged with perjury or found to be a highly unreliable
rmant," neither of which was true. So much for not using
data.

eloquin admitted that he had defended the London *Daily*
*' * in a libel suit brought by Bally Corporation. The burden
he paper's defense was that Bally had mob connections—
rdo Catena had once been part owner. The paper won the
Nobody asked Peloquin why, if he had once defended a
using as the basis mob connections at Bally, he had al-
d Resorts to deal with Bally, as it often had over the years.
n February 20, shortly following the completion of Pelo-
's testimony, Resorts rested its case. It was the division's
There were only eight days left until Resorts' final tempo-
permit ran out, and the governor was putting pressure on.

casinos in Kentucky. They were as wide open as Resorts was
down the street. Nobody asked Peloquin why it was, then, that
gambling interests had to blackmail an anti-casino would-be
sheriff to keep him from winning.

Peloquin was grilled on the subject of Eddie Cellini. Peloquin wrote a letter to the Bahamian government in 1972—in
response to the government's allegation that Cellini was still on
the payroll—in which he said Cellini was severed in 1969.
Mickey Brown pointed out that not only had Cellini been paid
through 1970, but in 1970 he had gone on a fact-finding tour
of another casino for Resorts. Peloquin said he had forgotten
about that when he wrote the letter.

He had also forgotten to fire a man named Peter Hayes, who
had been "telephonically" linked to Canadian mobster Albert
Volpe. Peloquin said they had kept Hayes on because they
didn't want to blow the continuing wiretap on Volpe. Mickey
Brown pointed out that that was many years before. Peloquin
said he had forgotten about Peter Hayes until the Gaming
Enforcement report came out; then he fired him.

Peloquin gave a couple of speeches about how dangerous it
is to use "raw data"—for example, background information on
people that might include unsubstantiated charges. There was
a damaging file on Eddie Cellini found at Intertel, but Peloquin said it contained "raw data" and was disregarded.

There was a memo dealing with the relationship between Sy
Alter and Huntington Hartford. A confidential source advised
Intertel that in 1965, while still employed by Huntington Hartford, Sy Alter sought out two New York police detectives and
asked them to check to see if Hartford's home phone was
tapped, as Hartford thought. The report pointed out that the
two policemen were "rogue cops" who were later sent to prison
on felony charges. The source stated that during the period
involved, both Alter and Hartford were considered by persons

in police circles as "sick." They were, said the report, "sex degenerates who were the targets of many complaints by various women who came into contact with them."

The report went on to say that at least one other person connected with the incident was of the opinion, in retrospect, that Alter and the two detectives were working together, "engaged in a rip-off of Huntington Hartford." He said the two cops were rip-off artists who eventually were apprehended. One of the cops had a promising career, but it went sour when he amassed large gambling debts. He went to Florida and was jailed as a result of some "stickups" he participated in there. The source had a vague recollection that Alter had been loan sharking in New York in the mid-sixties and might be connected with the two cops in Florida. One of the two cops later committed suicide.

Peloquin told the hearing that he had dismissed the whole thing as a shakedown of Alter. When Mickey Brown pushed further, Peloquin said, "The shame of reading a report like this —and it's as slanderous a type of thing as you can do—I'm ashamed to read the thing. When we talk about raw information or raw data, this is just what we're talking about. I probably grossly injured three or four people's lives by reading something like this."

As for Alter's attempted bribe of a New York judge, involving Hartford's liquor-store license, Peloquin said, "I think the information on Mr. Alter . . . was that he was an average citizen that got caught in a bind." There were other potentially embarrassing Peloquin memos. In one memo he wrote at Justice, he said that Stafford Sands, in his role as private attorney, had represented the majority of racketeer interests "we've identified in the Bahamas."

Mickey Brown questioned Peloquin about Vincent Teresa's testimony that to run a junket to Paradise Island, you had to go through Meyer Lansky and Dino Cellini, and about Teresa's

allegations that Peloquin had tried to bribe him ou ing against Resorts (in the *Rolling Stone* libel suit) him a job. Peloquin denied both stories. He said had a reputation in law enforcement circles as " grossest liars that ever came down the pike." F Teresa was the reason the government lost its b against Meyer Lansky and Dino Cellini. He said Edward Harrington, the government counsel in and now U.S. attorney for Boston—what he thoug Harrington, he claimed, said Teresa was a liar. D state produced an affidavit from Harrington th least twenty individual defendants were convicte of testimony by Vincent C. Teresa in various fe . . . I have never called Vincent Teresa a liar, but him to be a credible witness in the criminal ca was involved."

On another occasion, Peloquin testified that sion report came out in December of 1978, I Cellini whether a point concerning Dino wa; Eddie called Dino and reported back that it wa problem with that one, the state told Peloquin had been dead for some time before the state r Peloquin was stumped. He came back after th he had called Eddie and cleared it up. Eddie ha after he was first interviewed by the division

Another subject discussed was a 1971 article tel that appeared in the Las Vegas *Sun*. T Witwer, a former PR man in the Bahamas, other things, that Intertel was mob-linked association with Resorts International. Pelo newspaper's publisher, Hank Greenspun, I article. But the retraction was never prin which would seem to negate the point of Greenspun, when I called and asked him,

If the permit expired, the casino would be run by conservators. The governor publicly took the commission to task for not working long enough hours. Al Merck called the governor's interference "improper." He said they couldn't hurry through important hearings "to accommodate the tax collector."

Joseph Lordi told state lawyer Mickey Brown that he didn't care what, if anything, the state had left in its bag of tricks, he wanted them to finish before the expiration. It was as if a judge in a criminal trial gave the defense unlimited time to make its case, then gave the prosecution only one week.

But it might not have mattered anyway, because the state didn't have much to offer. The division questioned a few of its investigators on how they handled the case, on who wouldn't talk, that sort of thing. Then they slapped on the stand James Hawthorne, a convict from Florida who had a police record several pages long, including much illegal gambling activity. The amazing thing was that the state had decided not to put on Donna Wilson because she had slept with Crosby, but instead put on a man who, for example, said he changed his name every time he got married and told of how once, on the lam in Germany, he was awakened at dawn by CIA men who dragged him to the airport and put him on a plane to New York, where he was arrested.

Hawthorne said he was an undercover agent for Scotland Yard—New Jersey insists that is true—and that once he was doing surveillances in the Bahamas. Ray Brown asked who he was "surveilling," and Hawthorne said it was confidential. Ray Brown said he must answer. Lordi said he must answer. Mickey Brown said that Lordi had not made Probinsky answer a similar question. Lordi said, "Yes, but he told us in open why he wasn't going to." So Hawthorne said that he couldn't because "it's confidential information which the British government doesn't care to have made available to the public." Ray Brown said, "The British government doesn't. God save the queen!" The hearing room howled. Mickey Brown said, "I don't think we need these comments, Mr. Ray Brown." Ray Brown said, "You've got it whether you like it or not." Mickey said, "What is this, a joke?" Lordi said, "The question is whether I like it or not and I don't like it." Ray Brown said, "I can understand the preferences in this courtroom."

Lordi: "And you can stop characterizing the witness's testimony."

Ray Brown: "Michael Brown can hang from the ceiling and swing—"

Lordi: "Mr. Brown, let's maintain a little order. We know exactly where we are."

Then Lordi instructed the witness to answer the question. Hawthorne said they had Stafford Sands under surveillance, as well as Sir Roy Solomen and some Resorts officials. The only one of the latter he knew for sure was Jack Davis, but he wasn't on that case himself, so he didn't know what they found out.

The point of Hawthorne's testimony was supposed to be that he was friendly with the Cellini brothers and knew as fact that Eddie Cellini was involved with Meyer Lansky. No one seemed to care about the seemingly credible things Hawthorne had to say because they were too diluted by the incredible.

Then came the summations, on day thirty of hearings, with, as Mickey Brown pointed out, five hundred documents in evidence. Mickey Brown questioned the credibility of Resorts' excuses in a talk that carried the theme Do you believe this? Ray Brown spent a lot of his summation talking about what a lousy witness Hawthorne had been. The inference was clear: If that was all the state had to offer, how could you believe any of it? Ray Brown made much mention of the profitability of Resorts' casinos. He also said, "Not a dime of any money that came in here could be considered improper or unclean."

When it was all over, Merck requested a finding of facts from both sides of the case, as is common in court trials. Lordi said no. Merck said there were eight thousand pages of testimony to be reviewed. Lordi said all the other commissioners seemed to feel equipped to handle it themselves. Merck began to push the point, and Lordi said, "Let the record show that you are the one who is wasting time." It was one more flare-up in a relationship that even publicly was barely civil. It was Friday. The commissioners had two days to reach a verdict.

CHAPTER THIRTY-SIX

On Monday morning, February 26, a man from the Dow-Jones wire service rushed into the *Barron's* offices and exclaimed that a friend of his had just bought some stock in Resorts International because on New Jersey UHF television, Lordi was saying how great Resorts was—the friend said it was obvious they were going to get a license.

Indeed, at that moment Joseph Lordi was reading a seventy-two-page, almost two-hour statement in which he said that "the applicant has demonstrated its ability to properly operate the casino in conformance with the strict New Jersey regulations." Resorts, he said, "has established by clear and convincing evidence its financial stability, the integrity and responsibility of its financial backers, its good reputation for honesty and integrity, and its business ability." Lordi said Resorts had become "effective and dedicated enemies" of organized crime. Not only that, he added, but "their name became anathema to organized crime." Lordi cast his vote in favor of granting Resorts a permanent license.

Then he threw the ball to the rest of the commissioners. The courtroom was tense. The press had already cast its vote in large part: editorials had become increasingly negative. The people of New Jersey had cast a kind of vote too. In a poll only weeks earlier, an overwhelming majority said they thought Resorts was run by organized crime. A requirement of the casino law was that the companies running the casino have the public trust. Would the commission observe that law? Only the licensing vote would tell.

Then it came. Kenneth McDonald said yes. Alice Corsey, cute to the end, asked, "What are we voting on?" Then she said that "a few lingering questions about the allegations . . . undoubtedly will always remain, but when balanced against the weight of credible evidence, no reasonable person could say Resorts International, Inc., is not suitable to be the state's first licensed casino operator." Then she voted yes. Prospero DeBona noted that it was not a permanent license being proposed but, rather, a "plenary" license that would have to be renewed from time to time. Then he said yes.

All eyes were on Al Merck. He was the only one who tried to hinge approval on conditions being met. He called for establishment of an independent audit committee on Resorts' board of directors to oversee accounting functions. He wanted to require Resorts to build a hotel it had promised. He wanted Sy Alter permanently off the Resorts payroll. There were audible boos in the hearing room as Merck spoke. Lordi said no to all the proposals, and the other three commissioners bobbed their heads in agreement. Lordi said, in effect, that we can't tell these people how to run their business. When it came his turn to vote, Merck hesitated, a long, painful silence, his jaw tensely working. Then he said yes.

The hearing room erupted into cheers from the out-in-force Resorts contingent. Lawyers hugged lawyers, dealers danced around, and the newspapers the next day showed Jack Davis watching it all, wearing his version of a smile.

Media editorials from Florida to Philadelphia were heavily weighted against the decision. *The New York Times* said that if the New Jersey governor and the legislature were to study the hearings, "They will have to face up to the fact that cities and states that rely on profits from gambling find it difficult to be overly fastidious about who supplies them." CBS-TV gave a short editorial course to anyone who wants to run a casino in Atlantic City: "You should know it's okay to have employees who gained their experience in illegal gambling operations . . . to have kept employees on the payroll even after you had good reason to suspect they had connections with organized crime . . . to have given payments to officials of a foreign country where you had a casino, and to have improperly recorded these payments on your company's books. . . . The trick is to admit these things and say sure, you did them, but that you don't do them anymore." That same editorial summed up a prevailing sentiment on Lordi's blue-sky final opinion: "It's disturbing to us that the Casino Control Commission has granted this company a permanent license without condition, without even a word of warning about future behavior. Instead, Chairman Joseph Lordi gave the commission's blessing to Resorts, saying, 'Resorts has established by clear and convincing evidence its good reputation for honesty and integrity.' They have to be kidding."

To be sure, there were some editorials, and obviously some individuals, that supported the decision. Three days after it was all over, a postcard, the chicken-scrawl variety, arrived in *Barron's* offices. It read: "ha ha ha ha ha ha ha ha ha ha ha ha ha ha ha ha ha you F—— harpies." Like most mail from Resorts' fans, it was not signed.

CHAPTER THIRTY-SEVEN

Toward the end of the Resorts' hearings, commissioner Kenneth McDonald asked prosecutor G. Michael Brown if the state had any evidence to indicate Resorts International was currently linked to organized crime. Brown said they did not, but he said that clearly there had been such associations in the past. McDonald, with his "yes" vote—and like his fellow commissioners—showed he didn't care what had gone on in the past. He voted for the present.

It may be that there is a "new" Resorts International that is above reproach, but it seems unlikely that the character of a company could change any more than a person's could. In the months that followed the verdict, Resorts carried on in its usual arrogant way and controversy continued to be its ever-loyal companion.

Within a month of the verdict in Atlantic City, Brigitte Davis, long-neglected wife of Resorts president Jack Davis, was found dead in an apartment in Miami's Jockey Club. The company called it a heart attack. The coroner's report called it suicide—an overdose of sedatives. The report said she had been dead for several days before she was found.

The police report was confused. It seemed that when she was finally found, one person was on the scene so fast it was assumed he was a security guard or a cop. He turned out to be Raymond Gore, financial vice-president of Resorts International.

Not long after the license verdict, David Probinsky announced he was running for mayor of Atlantic City. A *New York Times* editorial suggested he use the campaign slogan "Clean up in Atlantic City."

In mid-1979, following his Iranian getaway, the Shah of Iran showed up on Paradise Island and moved into James Crosby's Agent 007–like barbed-wire-ringed residence. (I once asked a Bahamian taxi driver what he thought of all that barbed wire. "Man got to have his privacy," he replied.) The Shah's visit revived the rumors about Resorts being linked to the CIA (the trip was perhaps arranged by sometime Paradise Island visitor Henry Kissinger) and gave rise to local headlines like SHAH BUYS OCEAN CLUB? Locals guessed that the Shah was headed for Mexico next, because Intertel operatives were suddenly flying off in that direction. As it turned out, the Shah was headed for Mexico next.

Within six months of the Boardwalk verdict, Resorts was labeled "Boardwalk bully," even by former supporters. License in hand, the company was resorting to its old ways, trying to gain control of the tram that ran up and down the Boardwalk. It got control, over objections of the local chamber of commerce, which feared Atlantic City was becoming a "company town." There is ongoing unrelated but equally arrogant behavior. People visiting the casino have made a table count and found that the two- and five-dollar-minimum tables are rarely the required percentage of total.

Not quite a year following the verdict, the Division of Gaming Enforcement hit Resorts with a number of credit violation charges. The list of names of people who received special—and illegal—credit favors was sealed, but Lucinda Fleeson, a *Bergen Record* reporter, eventually got hold of it. Among the violators was New Jersey Assemblyman Michael Matthews, from Atlantic City.

Resorts continues to draw other law enforcement attention. It was announced that the SEC is investigating the adequacy of the company's disclosures to that agency since 1970. And the Bahamian government, too, said it was launching an investigation of its own in light of revelations at the New Jersey hearings.

Despite it all, Resorts International apparently is not deterred. In mid-1979, an Albany banker told me that Resorts had sent a lawyer to Saratoga, New York, to expound on the joys of bringing casino gambling to your hometown. James Crosby has said that if casinos come to New York and Florida, his company will be there. At this writing, there are published reports that Resorts has optioned land in Coney Island.

Meanwhile, events are unfolding in Florida that are hauntingly familiar. A Miami source claims that $4 million is being funneled into a new pro-casino drive in that city. The figure is without verification and may be high—it shouldn't take that much. In early 1979, G. Wilson Purdy was fired from his post as chief of the Dade County, Florida, Department of Public Safety by Merrett Stierheim, the county commissioner. The official reason had to do with pressures over confrontations between white policemen and the black community. It's tough to find an investigator from the department's organized-crime division who buys that explanation. Wilson Purdy was one of the driving forces behind the defeat of the 1978 Florida casino referendum. He had put the considerable resources of his organized-crime department into the anti-casino effort.

When Purdy was fired, his successor, Bobby L. Jones, began a brick-by-brick dismantlement of the organized-crime section because, the department felt, organized crime was a federal problem. They said cops were needed more on the streets, keeping law and order. Some experienced organized-crime investigators were told to get into uniform and back onto the streets. One was given a job looking after library files. Many have quit. Dade County's organized-crime-fighting capacity has been drastically cut, and one of the most effective anti-casino voices has been stilled.

In New York, too, there has been at least one casino-connected dismissal. New York City Mayor Edward Koch fired Bernard Rome, head of the Off-Track Betting Corporation, when Rome came out in strong opposition to Koch's pro-casino stance. Rome said casinos were being railroaded through without adequate public hearings, and he called Koch arrogant. Koch replaced him with John Keenan, who may or may not agree with the mayor. Keenan was asked to come up with recommendations on gambling. He released a report that led many to wonder exactly which side he was on. It favored casinos, but then recommended restrictions that casino companies would never be willing to live with (as if they wouldn't beat them down anyway). It also detailed the negatives. For example, the report said that casinos would be a form of regressive taxation, since it would be mostly New Yorkers, and often poor minorities, who would be losing at the tables. It also suggested casinos might lead to an increase in New York's already hideously overburdened welfare roles, and might push the crime rate up in casino areas.

Proponents of casinos in Newport, Rhode Island, are using economic arguments, which comes at first as a surprise, considering Newport is known as one of America's wealthiest communities. The problem is, Newport is largely a summer community whose financial base is tourists—who are there only three months of the year. Also, the city itself supports the upkeep of a number of huge white elephants of mansions, which have burdened its coffers. Would-be casino owners (the prime mover, incidentally, lives in Massachusetts) claim the city's fiscal problems would be ended if only it had casinos.

A more novel argument comes from Chicago Mayor Jane Byrne, who sees casinos as a solution for snow. In mid-1979, the mayor suggested that perhaps a well-placed casino or two, maybe one on a boat in Lake Michigan, would offset budgetary problems caused by an overabundance of snow the winter before.

On it goes. Build a casino, clothe the elderly, feed the poor, balance the budget. Those are the promises of social betterment, but the promises have yet to be fulfilled. It can be argued, for example, that the elderly and the poor of Atlantic City are worse off than before. And the costs mount. New Jersey's attorney general notes that in the first six months of 1979, Atlantic City led the nation in growth of crime. And, too, no one has found a way to keep organized crime out. So what? If there are going to be casinos, it is an often-asked question, why not let the people who know how to run them, run them? Some law enforcement officials have a ready answer to that question. First, the obvious: the mob cannot be expected to operate casinos honestly. They cannot be expected to give the state its full share of the take. Then, too, goes the argument, organized crime is not content to confine itself to casinos. They use the vast amounts of cash to corrupt once-legitimate businesses, to infiltrate institutions and to bribe politicians.

Besides, add the enforcers, stressing organized crime is begging another issue. There are few companies that go into gam-

bling for altruistic reasons. The casino business does not attract
the IBMs of the world. The standards set by casinos are much
lower than those expected of the rest of society. There are few
better cases in point than Resorts International. The company
dealt with the mob when it was expedient to do so. It paid off
political leaders to obtain political favors. It explains that these
things were legal in the Bahamas, but if Resorts sets low standards for itself in the islands, what's to stop it from doing the
same in Atlantic City or Florida or New York? Likewise, if
Caesar's World ignores Nevada orders to stop dealing with
unsavory characters, who will it listen to in New Jersey, where
it has already opened a casino? Bally, the third casino to open
in New Jersey, has admitted it once employed Meyer Lansky
aide Dino Cellini. To save its own hide in Atlantic City, Resorts International went to great pains to show it had never
dealt with that Cellini. Those happen to be the first three
casino companies to hit New Jersey, and every one of them has
something in its past that would be considered unacceptable
in most other businesses.

So who will be next? Who will bribe whom and where?
Which organized-crime figure will get the laundry business and
which the vending machines? What company will appear with
what dark secret in its past? And once they all get there and
wield their strong influence on those around them, turning
cities into company towns and states into company states, what
will be the result? Will people lose not only at the tables but
in ways they never dreamed? Will they continue to lose the
idealistic investigators—the Dennis Gomes—and suffer in
their place men whose motives are questionable? Will they lose
the legitimate businesses and have incorporated into their
economy the higher costs of doing business with organized
crime? If the answers to those questions is yes, then it must
follow, too, that the character of the society they live in will
be eroded.

Two New Jersey state senators traveled to Paradise Island in April of 1977, ostensibly to see how gambling operated there, and were greeted by a storm of protest upon their return. For one thing, they had been treated to free dinners, deep-sea fishing and scuba-diving lessons by Resorts International. Second, even though part of their trip seemed to be a boondoggle —all that fishing and diving could not have left much time for investigating—one of the senators intended to present the state senate with a bill for all of his noncomplimentary expenditures. The other agreed to pay his own way. He was State Senator Joseph Maressa of Camden, and he said, "I don't see anything wrong with it, but this is an election year and I'm not going to get myself in trouble for a lousy three or four hundred dollars."

By January 1980, Joseph Maressa may have gotten himself in trouble for a whole lot more. He was one of the alleged flies caught in the giant Abscam web of the FBI. Maressa allegedly told undercover FBI agents—who were masquerading as representatives of an Arab businessman trying to get into Atlantic City—that he had considerable influence over the Casino Control Commission. He also allegedly took at least $10,000 in legal fees, saying it was "almost patriotic" to do so.

And it is now history that the New Jersey Casino Control Commission was directly implicated in Abscam. Commissioner Kenneth McDonald reportedly was one of two men—the other was Mayor Angelo Errichetti of Camden—who received $100,000 in return for future favors to the Arab. (Errichetti, incidentally, hired himself a good lawyer: Raymond Brown.) Casino Control Commission chairman Joseph Lordi said that McDonald was "suckered." But Governor Byrne forced McDonald to resign his post, and instructed Attorney General John Degnan to investigate.

Nor did Lordi himself emerge unscathed. New Jersey Senator Harrison "Pete" Williams allegedly told undercover agents that he had intervened with Lordi to get a would-be casino operator, Ritz Associates, a building variance that saved them $3 million. Lordi hotly denied it.

On February 11, 1980, Governor Byrne announced that in order to "begin restoring the public confidence" in New Jersey's casino gambling industry, he was proposing strengthening the laws. He wanted to abolish part-time commissioners and substitute a full-time five-member commission, with each member paid $60,000 a year. He did not address the problem of how he would insure they were honest. (Following McDonald's resignation, the governor was hard-pressed to find anyone who would take the job.)

The governor also called for new ethics laws prohibiting state officials from accepting employment with casinos for two years after leaving their posts. He didn't suggest that those who had already done so be asked to resign. He further said it was time to call a halt to granting temporary casino permits. By that time, three had been granted, to Resorts, Caesar's World and Bally. Byrne did not comment on whether he thought such permits had been a mistake in the first place. After Byrne unveiled his proposals, the state legislature got down to the business of amending casino law. They were immediately embroiled in politics. A powerful committee head in the assembly, Richard Codey, refused to let through any legislation that did not specifically designate his fellow Essex County Democrat Joseph Lordi as continuing on the Casino Control Commission. Eventually Lordi was allowed to serve out his term, and four new commissioners were appointed. Three were from New Jersey, one from Washington, D.C., which led to the inevitable joke: they couldn't find four honest people in the state of New Jersey. Temporary permits were not abolished, as the governor at first suggested.

The public reaction to Abscam in New Jersey ranged from outrage that officials could be so easily bought to resigned acceptance of such doings by politicians. There was other predictable sentiment. Members of Congress and the Washington press corps found the FBI's tactics scurrilous. (Though no one in Congress ever complained when the same "sting" tactics were used on drug dealers and record counterfeiters.) Some members of Congress further decried the fact that the story had been leaked to the news media before any indictments were handed down. The Justice Department reacted by appointing Connecticut U.S. Attorney Richard Blumenthal to determine where the leaks had occurred. And all the fuss about "leaks" and "timing" was beside the main point—that leading government officials were, allegedly, once again "on the take," Watergate notwithstanding.

Whichever side one takes, one must face the inevitable questions. There are the specific ones: Was it the first time a commissioner had taken a bribe—if indeed one had? Had they done so in real life, not just in an FBI sting? Was Lordi, as implied, susceptible to political favor-doing, and if so, had he done favors in the past?

There are broader issues, of course. Is it possible to find

honest men and women to police gambling in an uninfluenced way, despite casino interests willing to spread around millions of dollars? Or is it inevitable that where there is gambling, there will also be public corruption on a massive scale? If an industry controls a state and, for example, a United States senator, does its influence then extend into policy making at the federal level, and thus, really, into every state?

Signs are, the answers to those questions will be hard to live with.

INDEX

Abelson, Alan, 20, 23
Abplanalp, Robert, 33
Abscam scandal, 247–50
    FBI tactics in investigation of, 249
    implications of, 250
    public reaction to, 249
    Resorts International and, 247
Aladdin Hotel and Casino, as example of gambling law enforcement, 145
Allen, Stu, 43
All the President's Men (Woodward and Bernstein), 35
Alter, Seymour, 33, 34, 37–38, 39, 40, 50, 65–66, 78, 81, 82, 83, 107, 116, 117, 146, 197, 209, 212, 216, 218, 219, 220, 221, 226, 228, 231, 232, 239
American National Life Insurance Company, 215
Aranow, Peter, 178
Argent Corporation, 143, 144
Arrington, Henry, 85, 88
Atlantic City
    black and Hispanic voting block in, referendum on gambling and, 15–16
    blacks, effects of gambling on, 180
    casino stocks and, 165–70
    churches in, effects of gambling on, 186
    Committee to Rebuild, 15, 123, 124
    construction industry in, 187
    crime rate, rise of, as effect of gambling, 184–86
    early history of, 14
    Hispanic population in, effects of gambling on, 179–80
    illegal practices by Resorts' casino management, 174–76
    landmarks, destruction of, for casino hotels, 179
    opening day of gambling in, 163–64
    organized crime in, 17, 184–86
    Penthouse incident and, 181–82
    property values in, after introduction of gambling, 187
    Resorts International's early interest in, 120–24, 126, 127

ABOUT THE AUTHOR

GIGI MAHON is an associate editor and
feature writer at *Barron's* financial weekly
and a monthly columnist for *Mademoiselle*
magazine. A graduate of the Boston
University School of Public Communication,
she lives in the New York area.